This Book Belongs to:

_____

Carrot-Praline Cake,
page 126

Christmas Cookbook

Filled to the brim with 191 holiday recipes, menus & easy-to-make treats for sharing!

Oxmoor HOUSE®

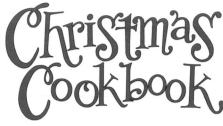

©2004 by Gooseberry Patch,
600 London, Delaware, Ohio 43015,
www.gooseberrypatch.com
©2004 by Oxmoor House, Inc.
Book Division of Southern Progress Corporation
P. O. Box 2262, Birmingham, Alabama 35201-2262

Hardcover ISBN: 0-8487-2840-8
Softcover ISBN: 0-8487-2870-X
Library of Congress Control Number: 2004112820
Printed in the United States of America
Eighth Printing 2007

OXMOOR HOUSE, INC.
Editor in Chief: Nancy Fitzpatrick Wyatt
Executive Editor: Susan Carlisle Payne
Art Director: Cynthia Rose Cooper
Copy Chief: Allison Long Lowery

Gooseberry Patch Christmas Cookbook
Editor: Kelly Hooper Troiano
Editorial Assistant: Shannon Friedmann
Senior Photographer: Jim Bathie
Photographer: Brit Huckabay
Senior Photo Stylist: Kay E. Clarke
Photo Stylists: Amy Wilson, Ashley J. Wyatt
Director, Test Kitchens: Elizabeth Tyler Luckett
Assistant Director, Test Kitchens: Julie Christopher
Test Kitchens Staff: Kristi Carter, Nicole Lee Faber,
    Kathleen Royal Phillips, Jan A. Smith, Elise Weis,
    Kelley Self Wilton
Publishing Systems Administrator: Rick Tucker
Color Specialist: Jim Sheetz
Director of Production: Phillip Lee
Production Manager: Theresa L. Beste
Production Assistant: Faye Porter Bonner

Contributors:
Copy Editor: Lauren Brooks
Designer: Connie Formby
Editorial Intern: Jessica Lynn Dorsey
Indexer: Mary Ann Laurens

To order additional publications,
call 1-800-765-6400.
For more books to enrich your life, visit
oxmoorhouse.com

Cranberry-Ginger
Crumble Cake, page 128

Contents

Holiday Greetings from Vickie & Jo Ann

Dear Friend,

As your neighbors at Gooseberry Patch, we love tradition as much as you do, and we know there's no time like Christmas to celebrate ways to make this magical season the best that it can be. We've created this holiday cookbook with just that in mind. Our **Gooseberry Patch Christmas Cookbook** is full of mouthwatering recipes, holiday photographs, gift-giving ideas and cooking tips...just for you. We want to help make your holidays easier than ever!

As you peek through these pages, you'll find our very favorite recipes like Cranberry Applesauce, Party Rosemary Pork, Holiday Yams, Peppermint Candy Ice Cream Pie and Eggnog Cookies. And don't miss our Goodies for Giving...Ho-Ho Cocoa Mix, Herbal Cheese Spread, Apple Cobbler in a Jar and Slice & Bake Sugar Cookies will make everyone on your gift list happy.

The Christmas season is a time for sharing our hearts and homes with those we love most. For those of us who enjoy country living, the season is best enjoyed when we surround ourselves with good food, family & friends. The time we spend baking and wrapping food gifts is rewarded by the smiles on the faces of those with whom we share. This year let our **Gooseberry Patch Christmas Cookbook** help you and your family usher in the holidays with warmth, with joy, with laughter and love.

Vickie &
JoAnn

Clockwise from top left:
Broccoli Cornbread,
Poinsettia Punch and White
Bean Chili, page 35

Our Favorite Christmas Menus

★

Hosting a holiday meal at home is a gesture that family & friends will remember fondly. Celebrate the season with our happy gatherings...from a caroling party to a cookie swap.

Christmas Dinner with all the Trimmings

Peppered Beef Tenderloin, page 13

Savor this big Christmas dinner with your family. Begin with bowls of Butternut Squash Soup; then feast on flavorful slices of beef tenderloin with all the traditional side trimmings. For dessert, everyone will enjoy the decadent Double-Chocolate Christmas Praline-Fudge Cake with cheers of Wassail.

Menu

Butternut Squash Soup

Peppered Beef Tenderloin

Cornbread Dressing

Holiday Yams

Green Beans Supreme

Cranberry Applesauce

Double-Chocolate Christmas
Praline-Fudge Cake

Wassail

Serves
6 to 8

Butternut Squash Soup

This velvety starter soup is a blend of pureed squash and carrots, cream and a hint of ginger.

3-lb. butternut squash
8 carrots, peeled and thickly
  sliced
2½ c. chicken broth
¾ c. orange juice
½ t. salt

½ t. ground ginger
½ c. whipping cream
2 T. finely chopped pecans,
  toasted
Nutmeg

Cut squash in half lengthwise; remove seeds. Place squash, cut sides down, in a shallow pan; add hot water to pan to depth of ¾ inches. Cover with aluminum foil and bake at 400 degrees for 40 minutes or until tender; drain. Scoop out pulp; mash. Discard shell. Cook carrots in boiling water 25 minutes or until tender; drain and mash.

Combine squash, carrots, chicken broth and next 3 ingredients in a bowl. Process half of mixture in a food processor or blender until smooth. Repeat procedure with remaining half of squash mixture.

Place pureed mixture in a large saucepan; bring to a simmer. Stir in cream; return to a simmer. Remove from heat. To serve, ladle soup into individual bowls and sprinkle with pecans and nutmeg. Makes 8 cups.

Peppered Beef Tenderloin

(pictured on page 11)

8-oz. container sour cream
3 T. Dijon mustard
2 T. prepared horseradish
2 T. whole green peppercorns
2 T. whole red peppercorns
2 t. coarse salt
3½- to 4-lb. beef tenderloin, trimmed

1 c. chopped fresh flat-leaf parsley
¼ c. butter or margarine, softened
3 T. Dijon mustard
Garnish: baby artichokes, fresh rosemary sprigs

For hotter flavor, substitute the more common black peppercorns for the less pungent green and red peppercorns.

Combine first 3 ingredients. Cover and chill.

Place peppercorns in a blender; cover and process until chopped. Transfer to a bowl and stir in salt.

Place beef on a lightly greased rack in a shallow roasting pan. Combine parsley, butter and 3 tablespoons mustard; rub mixture evenly over beef. Pat peppercorn mixture evenly over beef. Cover and chill up to 24 hours.

Bake at 350 degrees for 50 minutes or until a meat thermometer inserted in thickest portion of beef registers 145 degrees (medium-rare) to 160 degrees (medium). Transfer beef to a platter; cover loosely with aluminum foil. Let stand 10 minutes before slicing. Serve with sour cream mixture. Garnish, if desired. Makes 8 servings.

Cornbread Dressing

4 c. cornbread, cubed (See below)
2 c. bread, cubed
½ c. green pepper, chopped
1 c. onion, chopped
½ c. celery, chopped

2 (10-oz.) cans chicken broth
2 eggs, beaten
2 T. dried sage
Salt and black pepper to taste

Lay cornbread and bread on parchment paper overnight to dry. When ready to prepare dressing, gently toss cornbread and bread cubes with green pepper, onion, celery, chicken broth, eggs, sage, salt and pepper; blend well. Spoon in a greased 9"x9" baking dish and bake at 350 degrees for 45 minutes. Makes 6 to 8 servings.

To make Basic Cornbread, heat a well-greased 9" oven-proof skillet at 450 degrees for 5 minutes. Meanwhile, stir together 2 cups buttermilk self-rising white cornmeal mix, ½ cup all-purpose flour, ¼ cup butter or margarine, melted, one lightly beaten egg and 2 cups buttermilk. Pour batter into hot skillet and bake at 400 degrees for 20 minutes or until golden.

Holiday Yams

½ c. all-purpose flour
½ c. brown sugar, packed
½ c. quick-cooking oats, uncooked
1 t. cinnamon

⅓ c. butter or margarine, melted
2 (17-oz.) cans yams, drained
1 c. cranberries
1½ c. mini marshmallows

Combine flour, sugar, oats, cinnamon and butter until mixture resembles coarse crumbs. Measure out one cup, reserving remaining crumb mixture. Toss together reserved one cup crumb mixture, drained yams and cranberries. Place in a greased 8"x8" baking dish. Top with remaining crumb mixture.

Bake, uncovered, at 350 degrees for 35 minutes. Layer marshmallows on top and broil 4 to 5 inches from heat source for 2 to 3 minutes or until golden. Makes 6 to 8 servings.

Christmas Memories

"Each year, for our Christmas dinner table, we put a special favor at each person's place that they get to keep. Usually it's some sort of ornament for the tree that we have made."

–Jan Ertola

Green Beans Supreme

1 onion, sliced
1 T. fresh parsley, chopped
3 T. butter or margarine, divided
2 T. all-purpose flour
½ t. lemon zest
½ t. salt
⅛ t. pepper

½ c. milk
8-oz. container sour cream
2 (9-oz.) pkgs. frozen French-style
  green beans, cooked
½ c. shredded Cheddar cheese
¼ c. purchased plain bread crumbs

Cook onion and parsley in 2 tablespoons butter in a large skillet over medium heat until onion is tender. Blend in flour, lemon zest, salt and pepper. Stir in milk; heat until thick and bubbly. Add sour cream and green beans; heat thoroughly.

Spoon into an ungreased 2-quart baking dish; sprinkle with cheese. Melt remaining one tablespoon butter and toss with bread crumbs; sprinkle over bean mixture. Broil 3 to 4 inches from heat until golden. Makes 6 servings.

★ ★ ★

"This isn't your usual green bean casserole. Loaded with cheese and sour cream, it will be your new favorite!"
–SueMary Burford-Smith
Tulsa, OK

Cranberry Applesauce

¾ lb. cranberries
1½ c. water
¾ c. sugar

4 lbs. apples, cored and quartered
Garnish: cinnamon

Place cranberries, water, sugar and apples in a large saucepan. Cover and simmer for 20 minutes or until apples are soft. Cool slightly and press mixture through a sieve or food mill. Sprinkle with cinnamon before serving, if desired. Makes about 8 cups.

★

"So festive and colorful when spooned in a glass serving dish."
–Robbin Chamberlain
Worthington, OH

Wassail

3 c. sugar
9 c. water, divided
5 cinnamon sticks

6 c. cranberry juice
3 c. orange juice
3 T. lemon juice

Combine sugar, 3 cups water and cinnamon sticks in a large stockpot; boil for 10 minutes. Add cranberry juice, remaining water, orange juice and lemon juice; heat thoroughly. Remove cinnamon sticks before serving. Makes 20 servings.

Double-Chocolate Christmas Praline-Fudge Cake

(pictured on facing page)

*You can use 3 (9")
round cake pans for
this recipe. Bake layers
at 350 degrees for 18
to 22 minutes.*

1 c. butter or margarine	2 c. sugar
¼ c. baking cocoa	2 c. all-purpose flour
1 c. water	½ t. salt
½ c. buttermilk	Chocolate Ganache
2 eggs	Praline Frosting
1 t. baking soda	Garnish: chopped pecans
1 t. vanilla extract	

Cook first 3 ingredients in a saucepan over low heat, stirring constantly, until butter melts and mixture is smooth; remove from heat. Cool.

Beat buttermilk, 2 eggs, baking soda and vanilla at medium speed with an electric mixer until smooth. Add butter mixture to buttermilk mixture, beating until blended. Combine sugar, flour and salt; gradually add to buttermilk mixture, beating until blended. (Batter will be thin.)

Coat 3 (8") round cake pans with non-stick vegetable spray; line with wax paper. Pour batter evenly into pans. Bake at 350 degrees for 22 to 24 minutes or until set. Cool in pans on wire racks 10 minutes. Remove from pans and cool layers completely.

Spread about ½ cup ganache between cake layers; spread remainder on sides of cake only (not the top). Chill cake ½ hour. Pour frosting slowly over top of cake, spreading to edges, allowing some frosting to run over sides. Freeze, if desired; thaw at room temperature 4 to 6 hours. Garnish, if desired. Makes 10 to 12 servings.

Chocolate Ganache

2 c. semi-sweet chocolate chips	¼ c. butter or margarine, cut
⅓ c. whipping cream	into pieces

Microwave chocolate chips and cream in a glass bowl on medium power (50%) 2 to 3 minutes or until chips are melted. Whisk until smooth. Gradually add butter, whisking until smooth. Cool, whisking often, 15 to 20 minutes or until spreading consistency. Makes about 2 cups.

*This candy-like frosting
hardens very quickly, so
prepare it just before
frosting the cake.*

Praline Frosting

¼ c. butter or margarine	1 c. powdered sugar
1 c. light brown sugar, packed	1 t. vanilla extract
⅓ c. whipping cream	1 c. chopped pecans, toasted

Bring first 3 ingredients to a boil in a 2-quart saucepan over medium heat, stirring often; boil one minute. Remove from heat and whisk in powdered sugar and vanilla until smooth. Add toasted pecans, stirring gently 2 to 5 minutes or until frosting begins to cool and thicken slightly. Pour immediately over cake. Makes about 1¾ cups.

Christmas Eve Supper

★

Make this menu a part of your annual Christmas Eve tradition. Filled with shrimp and scallops, this rich casserole is a treat. Seasonal cranberries and toasted almonds complement the spinach in the salad. Don't forget the buttery dinner rolls...they're a highlight to this meal!

Menu

Rich Seafood Casserole

Cranberry-Spinach Salad

Holiday Dinner Rolls

Serves 8

Rich Seafood Casserole,
page 20

Rich Seafood Casserole

(pictured on page 19)

★ ★ ★

Fresh shrimp and scallops come to the table baked in a Swiss cheese and wine sauce that you can spoon over hot cooked rice. This dish can be made the day before. After assembling the casserole, cover and chill overnight. Let stand at room temperature 30 minutes before baking.

1½ lbs. unpeeled large fresh shrimp
1½ c. dry white wine
¼ c. chopped onion
¼ c. fresh parsley sprigs or celery leaves
1 T. butter or margarine
1 t. salt
1 lb. bay scallops
3 T. butter or margarine
3 T. all-purpose flour
1 c. half-and-half

½ c. shredded Swiss cheese
1 T. lemon juice
¾ t. lemon-pepper seasoning
7-oz. can sliced mushrooms, drained
1 c. freshly prepared whole-wheat bread crumbs
¼ c. grated Parmesan cheese
¼ c. sliced almonds
2 T. butter or margarine, melted
Hot cooked rice

Peel and, if desired, devein shrimp; set aside.

Combine wine and next 4 ingredients in a Dutch oven; bring to a boil. Add shrimp and scallops; cook 3 to 5 minutes or until shrimp turn pink. Drain shrimp mixture, reserving ⅔ cup broth.

Melt 3 tablespoons butter in Dutch oven over low heat; add flour, stirring until smooth. Cook, stirring constantly, one minute. Gradually add half-and-half; cook over medium heat, stirring constantly, until mixture is thickened and bubbly. Add Swiss cheese, stirring until cheese melts. Gradually stir in reserved ⅔ cup broth, lemon juice and lemon-pepper seasoning. Stir in shrimp mixture and mushrooms.

Spoon mixture into a lightly greased 11"x7" baking dish. Cover and bake at 350 degrees for 40 minutes. Combine bread crumbs and next 3 ingredients; sprinkle over casserole. Bake, uncovered, 10 minutes. Let stand 10 minutes before serving. Serve over rice. Makes 8 servings.

Christmas Memories

"Every Christmas Eve day my family and I go for a hayride on a wagon pulled by horses. We bundle up and take Christmas music along. As we are escorted through the snow in the crisp fresh air, we sing Christmas carols and ring big jingle bells we wear around our wrists. It's fun for the grandparents, parents, children and grandchildren. After the hayride, we drive back to Grandma's house for hot chili and cornbread."

—Amy McGrew
Miamisburg, OH

Cranberry–Spinach Salad

1 T. butter or margarine
¾ c. blanched, slivered almonds
1 lb. spinach, rinsed and torn
1 c. sweetened, dried cranberries
½ c. sugar
2 T. toasted sesame seeds

2 T. poppy seeds
2 t. minced onion
¼ t. paprika
½ c. vegetable oil
¼ c. white wine vinegar

Melt butter in a medium saucepan over medium heat. Sauté almonds in butter until lightly toasted; remove from heat, drain and let cool.

Toss spinach with toasted almonds and cranberries in a large bowl. Whisk together sugar, sesame seeds, poppy seeds, onion, paprika, oil and vinegar in a medium bowl. Toss with spinach mixture just before serving. Makes 8 to 10 servings.

Holiday Dinner Rolls

4 to 4½ c. all-purpose flour,
 divided
2 pkgs. active dry yeast
3 T. sugar

1 t. salt
1 c. milk
½ c. water
½ c. butter or margarine, divided

Combine 1½ cups flour, yeast, sugar and salt in a large mixing bowl.

Combine milk, water and ¼ cup butter (cut into chunks) in a medium-size heavy saucepan; cook over medium-low heat just until mixture reaches 120 degrees to 130 degrees. (Butter does not need to melt.) Gradually add milk mixture to flour mixture, beating at low speed with an electric mixer until smooth. Stir in enough remaining flour to make a soft dough.

Turn dough out onto a floured surface and knead until smooth and elastic (about 5 minutes). Place dough in a well-greased bowl, turning to grease top. Cover and let rise in a warm place (85 degrees), free from drafts, 30 minutes or until double in bulk. Punch dough down.

Divide dough into 18 equal portions; shape each portion of dough into a ball. Place balls into greased muffin cups. Cut an X-shape in tops of balls to make a cloverleaf. Cover and let rise in a warm place, free from drafts, 15 minutes or until double in bulk.

Melt remaining ¼ cup butter and brush rolls with butter. Bake at 375 degrees for 12 minutes or until lightly browned. Remove to wire rack to cool. Makes 18 rolls.

"These rolls are always the highlight of our holiday dinner. Just serve with apple butter for lots of smiles."

–Lara Shore
Independence, MO

For the Kids

If you don't eat the holiday meal until late afternoon, the kids may need snacks
to tide them over, so let them choose one (or all 3) of these tempting munchies. They're
easy enough that the kids can lend a helping hand in the kitchen. Watch out! You may find a few
adults sneaking a bite or two…so plan for extra!

Menu
Cheese Cookie Snacks

Pizza Snacks

Yummy Banana Pops

Serves 6 to 8

Cheese Cookie Snacks

1 c. shredded Cheddar cheese
½ c. butter or margarine, softened
1 c. all-purpose flour

¼ t. salt
1 c. crisp rice cereal

Stir together cheese and butter until blended. Stir in flour and salt; blend well. Stir in cereal. (Dough will be stiff.)

Shape dough into one-inch balls; place on an ungreased baking sheet 2 inches apart. Flatten cookies to ¼-inch thickness with a fork, making a crisscross pattern.

Bake at 350 degrees for 15 to 18 minutes. Remove to a wire rack to cool. Store in an airtight container. Makes about 2 dozen.

Pizza Snacks

(pictured on opposite page)

8-oz. can crescent rolls
6-oz. pkg. pepperoni slices
2 (1-oz.) mozzarella cheese sticks,
  cut into fourths

1 t. Italian seasoning
¼ t. garlic salt

Separate rolls into 8 triangles and place on a baking sheet. Place 2 pepperoni slices on each triangle; place one piece of cheese at wide end of triangle. Sprinkle with Italian seasoning. Roll up, starting at wide end. Sprinkle with garlic salt. Bake at 375 degrees for 10 to 12 minutes or until golden. Makes 8 snacks.

Yummy Banana Pops

4 small bananas, mashed
1 c. orange juice
2 T. sugar
2 T. water

1 t. lemon juice
6 (4-oz.) paper cups
6 wooden craft sticks

Combine first 5 ingredients. Place paper cups in a muffin pan. Spoon mixture into cups. Freeze one hour or until slightly firm; insert a stick in the center of each. Freeze 2 more hours or until firm. Peel off cups and serve. Makes 6 servings.

Breakfast with Santa

Mediterranean Coffee, Orange Streusel Muffins and Gingerbread Scones, page 26

Savor the joys of Christmas morning by making this oh-so simple breakfast. Sip on mugs of spiced coffee and nibble on warm scones and muffins while presents are being opened. After an exciting morning of fun and surprises, serve your hungry crowd a hearty casserole and fresh fruit.

Menu

Mediterranean Coffee

Gingerbread Scones

Orange Streusel Muffins

Fresh Strawberry and Orange Slices

Baked Sausage & Eggs

Serves 6

Mediterranean Coffee

(pictured on page 25)

¾ c. ground coffee
4 (3-inch) sticks cinnamon
1½ t. whole cloves
8 c. water
¼ c. chocolate syrup

⅓ c. sugar
½ t. anise extract
Whipped cream
Garnish: candy canes

Place ground coffee, cinnamon and cloves in a coffee filter or filter basket. Add water to coffeemaker and brew.

Stir syrup, sugar and anise into brewed coffee. Pour into mugs; top each with a dollop of whipped cream. Garnish, if desired. Makes 8 cups.

Gingerbread Scones

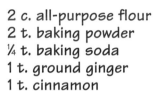

2 c. all-purpose flour
2 t. baking powder
¼ t. baking soda
1 t. ground ginger
1 t. cinnamon

¼ c. plus 3 T. unsalted butter,
   cut into pieces
⅓ c. molasses
⅓ c. milk

Combine first 5 ingredients; cut in butter with a pastry blender or 2 knives until mixture is crumbly. Combine molasses and milk; add to flour mixture, stirring just until dry ingredients are moistened. Turn dough out onto a lightly floured surface and knead lightly 4 or 5 times.

Divide dough in half; shape each portion into a ball. Pat each ball into a 5-inch circle on an ungreased baking sheet. Cut each circle into 6 wedges, using a sharp knife; do not separate wedges. Bake at 425 degrees for 10 to 12 minutes or until lightly browned. Serve warm. Makes one dozen.

Orange Streusel Muffins

(pictured on page 25)

2 c. all-purpose flour
2 t. baking powder
1 t. salt
⅓ c. sugar
½ c. chopped pecans
1 egg, lightly beaten
¼ c. orange juice
¼ c. milk

¼ c. vegetable oil
1 T. grated orange rind
½ c. orange marmalade
1 T. all-purpose flour
¼ c. sugar
½ t. cinnamon
¼ t. nutmeg
1 T. butter or margarine, softened

Combine first 5 ingredients in a large bowl; make a well in center of mixture. Set dry ingredients aside. Combine egg and next 5 ingredients; add to dry ingredients, stirring just until moistened. Spoon batter into greased muffins pans, filling pans ⅔ full.

Combine one tablespoon flour and remaining 4 ingredients; sprinkle over batter. Bake at 400 degrees for 17 minutes or until golden. Remove from pans immediately. Makes 15 muffins.

Baked Sausage & Eggs

6 breakfast sausage links
2 c. shredded sharp Cheddar
  cheese
1 T. all-purpose flour
1 c. shredded Monterey Jack
  cheese

6 eggs, lightly beaten
½ c. half-and-half
1 t. Worcestershire sauce

Cook sausage links according to package directions; drain on paper towels. Set sausage aside.

Combine Cheddar cheese and flour; sprinkle evenly in bottom of an ungreased 1½-quart shallow round baking dish. Sprinkle with Monterey Jack cheese and set aside.

Combine eggs, half-and-half and Worcestershire sauce; pour over cheese mixture. Arrange sausages on top of egg mixture in spoke fashion. Cover and chill 8 hours.

Remove from refrigerator. Let stand, covered, at room temperature 30 minutes. Bake, uncovered, at 350 degrees for 45 minutes or until set and lightly browned. Let stand 5 minutes before serving. Makes 6 servings.

Christmas Memories

"Granny used to make homemade biscuits for our family breakfast each Christmas morning. One year, we decided to save her the work and bought biscuits at a fast food restaurant the day before; however, not everyone in the family was in on this little secret. As we ate breakfast my cousin said, "Granny, these are the best biscuits you've ever made!" My how we all laughed! For the record, although she didn't use a recipe, Granny did make the best biscuits in the world."

–Robin Wilson
Altamonte Springs, FL

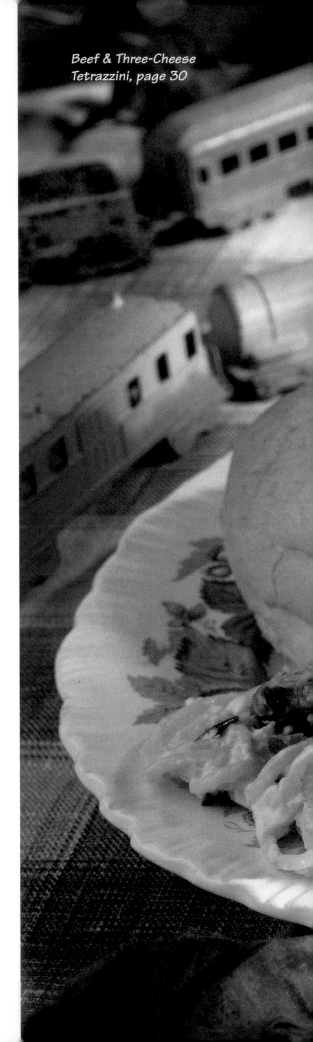

Beef & Three-Cheese Tetrazzini, page 30

Home for the Holidays

Welcome family home with a special dinner of all their favorite foods. After a sampling of this menu, we guarantee it'll make the top of the list year after year.

Menu

Beef & Three-Cheese Tetrazzini

Tossed Salad

Cheesy Bread or Plain Italian Bread

Peppermint Candy Ice Cream Pie

Serves 6 to 8

Beef & Three-Cheese Tetrazzini

(pictured on page 29)

★ ★ ★

Cream cheese and cottage cheese in the pasta provide a velvety contrast to the meaty sauce in this make-ahead dinner. Parmesan atop the pasta casserole completes the cheesy trio.

1½ lbs. ground chuck
½ c. chopped onion
1 t. salt
¼ t. pepper
15-oz. can tomato sauce
8-oz. linguine or spaghetti, uncooked

8-oz. pkg. cream cheese, softened
1 c. cottage cheese
¼ c. sour cream
¼ c. chopped green pepper
¼ c. sliced green onions
¼ c. freshly grated Parmesan cheese

Cook ground chuck and chopped onion in a large skillet over medium-high heat, stirring constantly, until meat crumbles. Drain.

Return meat and onion to skillet; add salt, pepper and tomato sauce. Cook 10 minutes over medium-low heat, stirring occasionally.

Cook linguine according to package directions. Drain and set aside.

Combine cream cheese, cottage cheese and sour cream; stir well. Stir in green pepper and green onions. Add linguine and stir well. Spoon linguine mixture into a greased 13"x9" baking dish. Pour meat sauce over top. Sprinkle with Parmesan cheese. Bake at 325 degrees for 30 minutes. Makes 6 to 8 servings.

Cheesy Bread

★

Melted cheese and a buttery sauce dress up store-bought bread, making an irresistible accompaniment to any pasta or soup dish. It's so good, you may need to make 2 loaves!

1 loaf bakery French bread
8-oz. pkg. sliced Swiss cheese
2 T. chopped onion
1 T. dry mustard

1 T. poppy seeds
1 t. seasoned salt
1 c. butter or margarine, melted

Cut diagonal slits into bread, using a serrated knife, cutting almost all the way through. Place bread on a large piece of aluminum foil and place on a baking sheet.

Place cheese slices in the slits. Combine onion and remaining 4 ingredients; drizzle over bread. Wrap foil around bread. Bake at 350 degrees for 35 to 40 minutes. Serve warm. Makes 6 to 8 servings.

Peppermint Candy Ice Cream Pie

1½ c. chocolate wafer crumbs
¼ c. plus 2 T. butter or margarine, melted
1 pt. peppermint ice cream
8-oz. frozen whipped topping, softened

3 T. peppermint candy, finely crushed
Garnish: additional peppermint candy

Combine chocolate wafer crumbs and melted butter; press firmly into a 9" pie plate. Combine peppermint ice cream and whipped topping; spoon into crumb crust. Sprinkle with peppermint candy; freeze until firm. Garnish with additional peppermint candy, if desired. Makes 6 to 8 servings.

Christmas Memories

"We have made a 'Past Christmases' photo album to take along to Grandma's house for the holidays. We've gathered all our Christmas photos taken over the years, and put them in an album, in no certain order. It's fun to look at the pictures and guess the years they were taken and what happened special that year."

—Melissa Hinte

Casual Weeknight Supper

*T*his simple menu is just the thing for those busy weeknights during the holiday hustle & bustle. Both the lasagna and cookies can be made ahead. But with chunky pieces of milk chocolate bars, these chocolate gems won't be around long!

Menu

Lasagna with Colorful Peppers

Buttered French Bread

Chewy Chunky
Chocolate-Walnut Cookies

Serves 8

Lasagna with Colorful Peppers

(pictured on opposite page)

12 lasagna noodles, uncooked
1 lb. sweet Italian sausage
½ lb. hot Italian sausage
1 large onion, sliced
2 red peppers, sliced
2 yellow peppers, sliced
2 green peppers, sliced
3 cloves garlic, chopped
½ c. fresh parsley, chopped
⅛ t. black pepper
8-oz. can tomato sauce
6-oz. can tomato paste
4 c. shredded part-skim
  mozzarella cheese
¼ c. grated Parmesan cheese

Italian sausage and red, green and yellow peppers mingle among the cheesy layers of this yummy lasagna.

Cook lasagna noodles according to package directions; drain well and set noodles aside.

Meanwhile, remove and discard casings from sausage. Cook sausage in a large skillet over medium heat until meat crumbles and is no longer pink; drain. Add onion, sliced peppers and garlic; cook over medium heat until vegetables are tender, stirring occasionally. Add parsley and black pepper.

Combine tomato sauce and tomato paste; stir well. Spread half of tomato sauce mixture in a lightly greased 13"x9" baking dish. Layer 4 lasagna noodles, half of sausage mixture, one cup mozzarella cheese and one tablespoon Parmesan cheese. Repeat noodle, sausage, and cheese layers. Top with remaining 4 lasagna noodles; spread remaining tomato sauce mixture over noodles. Top with remaining 2 cups mozzarella cheese; sprinkle with remaining 2 tablespoons Parmesan cheese. Bake, uncovered, at 350 degrees for 40 to 45 minutes. Let stand 15 minutes before serving. Makes 8 servings.

Chewy Chunky Chocolate-Walnut Cookies

1 c. butter or margarine, softened
¾ c. brown sugar, packed
½ c. sugar
1½ t. vanilla extract
1 egg
2¼ c. all-purpose flour
1 t. baking soda
½ t. salt
1½ c. coarsely chopped walnuts
  or pecans
2 (7-oz.) milk chocolate bars, cut
  into ½-inch pieces

Beat butter at medium speed with an electric mixer until creamy; gradually add sugars, beating well. Add vanilla and egg; beat well.

Combine flour, soda and salt; gradually add to butter mixture, beating well. Stir in walnuts and chocolate pieces.

Drop dough by rounded tablespoonfuls 2 inches apart onto ungreased baking sheets. Bake at 375 degrees for 10 minutes or until lightly browned. Cool slightly on baking sheets; remove to wire racks and let cool completely. Makes about 4 dozen.

Caroling Party

Warm up your fellow carolers with a batch of White Bean Chili...it's a nice change from traditional chili. Our cornbread and sweet punch keep the menu simple, giving everyone more time for encores of favorite Christmas melodies.

Menu

White Bean Chili

Broccoli Cornbread

Poinsettia Punch

Serves 12

White Bean Chili

(pictured on opposite page)

1 lb. dried Great Northern beans
2 medium onions, chopped
4 cloves garlic, minced
1 T. olive oil
2 (4.5-oz.) cans chopped green
   chilies, undrained
2 t. cumin
1½ t. dried oregano
⅛ t. red pepper

6 c. chicken broth
5 c. chopped cooked chicken
   breast
3 c. shredded Monterey Jack
   cheese, divided
Salt and black pepper to taste
Salsa
Sour cream
Garnish: chopped fresh parsley

In a hurry? To quick-soak dried beans, cover with water 2 inches above beans in a large Dutch oven. Bring to a boil; cover and cook 2 minutes. Remove from heat and let stand one hour. Drain.

   Sort and wash beans; place in a large Dutch oven. Cover with water 2 inches above beans; let soak 8 hours. Drain and set beans aside.

   Cook onion and garlic in oil in Dutch oven over medium-high heat, stirring constantly, until tender. Add green chilies and next 3 ingredients; cook 2 minutes, stirring constantly. Add beans and chicken broth. Bring to a boil; cover, reduce heat and simmer 2 hours or until beans are tender, stirring occasionally. Add chicken, one cup cheese and salt and pepper to taste. Bring to a boil; reduce heat and simmer, uncovered, 10 minutes, stirring often.

   Ladle chili into individual soup bowls. Top each serving evenly with remaining 2 cups cheese, salsa and sour cream. Garnish, if desired. Makes 13 cups.

Broccoli Cornbread

(pictured on page 8)

10-oz. pkg. frozen chopped
   broccoli, thawed
8½-oz. pkg. corn muffin mix
4 eggs, lightly beaten

1 c. cottage cheese
½ c. butter or margarine, melted
1 medium onion, minced
1 t. salt

   Drain broccoli, pressing between paper towels. Combine muffin mix and next 5 ingredients; stir. Add broccoli. Pour into a greased 13"x9" pan; bake at 400 degrees for 20 to 25 minutes or until golden. Cool; cut into squares. Makes 12 servings.

Poinsettia Punch

(pictured on page 8)

12-oz. can frozen pink lemonade
   concentrate, thawed and
   undiluted

2-ltr. bottle ginger ale, chilled
1 qt. raspberry sherbet, softened

Pink lemonade and raspberry sherbet is a zesty variation on the familiar lime sherbet punch for the holidays.

   Combine concentrate and ginger ale in a punch bowl, stirring gently. Add sherbet by heaping tablespoonfuls; stir gently. Serve immediately. Makes 13 cups.

Open House

Celebrate the holidays with your friends by hosting an open house. It's easy to have a fun-filled party when you plan ahead. And since most of these recipes can be made in advance, you'll have more time to spend with your guests and less time in the kitchen. Take a peek at our mouthwatering desserts that start on page 124.

Take a peek at our mouthwatering desserts that start on page 124.

Menu

Party Rosemary Pork

Quick & Cheesy Cocktail Swirls

Layered Cheese Torta

Serves 24

Party Rosemary Pork, page 38, and Layered Cheese Torta, page 39

Party Rosemary Pork

2 (3-lb.) rolled boneless pork loin
  roasts
⅓ c. olive oil
¼ c. dried rosemary
2 T. coarsely ground pepper
2 T. balsamic vinegar

2 t. kosher salt
¾ c. mustard with honey
¾ c. mayonnaise
6 dozen cocktail rolls
Garnish: fresh rosemary sprigs

Remove strings from roast and separate into 4 single roasts. Place roasts on a lightly greased rack in a large roasting pan. Bake, uncovered, at 350 degrees for 30 minutes.

Combine oil, rosemary, pepper, vinegar and salt; brush over pork. Bake, uncovered, 45 more minutes or until a meat thermometer inserted in thickest portion of pork registers 160 degrees. Remove from oven and let stand, covered, 10 minutes before slicing.

Combine mustard and mayonnaise. Cut pork into thin slices and serve on cocktail rolls with sauce. Garnish platter, if desired. Makes 24 appetizer servings.

Quick & Cheesy Cocktail Swirls

10 slices bacon, crisply cooked
  and crumbled
2 (3-oz.) pkgs. cream cheese,
  softened
¼ c. finely chopped onion

2 t. milk
2 (8-oz.) cans refrigerated
  crescent dinner rolls
Grated Parmesan cheese

Looking for a warm appetizer that won't keep you in the kitchen while your guests entertain themselves? These can be made ahead and refrigerated up to 2 hours before baking.

Combine bacon, cream cheese, onion and milk in a small bowl, stirring well; set aside.

Unroll one can of refrigerated dough; do not separate along ridges. Roll dough into a 15"x8" rectangle. Spread half of cheese mixture evenly over dough, leaving ½-inch margin at edges. Roll up dough, jellyroll fashion, starting at long side; pinch seams to seal. Cut dough into ½-inch slices; place slices, cut side down, on ungreased baking sheets. Sprinkle lightly with Parmesan cheese. Repeat with other can of dough and remaining cheese mixture.

Bake at 375 degrees for 12 to 15 minutes or until golden. Serve warm. Makes 5 dozen.

Layered Cheese Torta

7-oz. jar sun-dried tomatoes in oil, undrained
3 cloves garlic
2½ c. loosely packed fresh basil leaves
1 c. refrigerated finely shredded Parmesan cheese
¼ c. pine nuts, toasted
⅛ t. salt
⅛ t. pepper
⅓ c. olive oil
2 c. unsalted butter, softened
2 (8-oz.) pkgs. cream cheese, cut into one-inch cubes
Garnish: fresh basil leaves

Dried tomatoes and fresh basil create ribbons of holiday color in this rich appetizer cheese spread.

Lightly grease an 8½"x4½" loafpan. Line pan with plastic wrap, allowing it to extend slightly over edges of pan. Set pan aside.

Drain tomatoes, reserving 2 tablespoons oil. Process tomatoes and reserved oil in a food processor until minced. Transfer to a bowl; set aside. Wipe processor bowl with a paper towel.

Process garlic 5 seconds or until minced. Add basil, Parmesan cheese, pine nuts, salt and pepper; process until basil is finely chopped. Slowly add olive oil; process until mixture is smooth. Transfer mixture to a small bowl and set aside. Wipe processor bowl clean with a paper towel.

Process butter until light and fluffy, stopping once to scrape down sides. Add cream cheese cubes; process until smooth, stopping once to scrape down sides.

Spread one cup butter mixture evenly in prepared pan, smoothing with a spatula. Spread half of basil mixture over butter mixture; top with one cup butter mixture. Spread tomato mixture evenly over butter mixture. Spread one cup butter mixture evenly over tomato mixture. Top with remaining basil mixture and remaining butter mixture, smoothing each layer to edges of pan. Cover and chill at least 8 hours or up to 24 hours.

To serve, invert pan onto a serving platter; remove plastic wrap. Garnish, if desired. Serve with crackers. Makes 24 appetizer servings.

Christmas Memories

"While growing up on a farm in Pennsylvania, I could hardly wait for our family's annual Christmas barn party! It was always held on December 23rd and all our family and friends were invited. My 4 brothers and sisters, our cousins and I would rehearse the Nativity play that we would perform. Dad would set up bales of hay all over the barn, we'd decorate, then act out the Nativity. That night provided enough Christmas spirit to last us the whole year through and create more memories than I can count. Unfortunately, when my brothers, sisters and I went away to college, the tradition ended. But now, as we are having our own families, we are thinking of reviving the tradition in the old barn. We all feel that it would be even more special now to share it with our own children. Here's to getting that old barn ready and creating new memories for the next generation!"

—Meg Veno
Glenmoore, PA

Just Dessert

⭐

*I*ndulge festive party-goers this season with yummy sweet treats. From this dazzling selection, get a jump-start on your party by making the cake and custard for the trifle up to two days ahead. Then the day before, assemble the trifle and make your cookies and cheesecake. When planning your menu, include one of the punches and hot beverages found on pages 54-57.

Menu

Strawberry Holiday
Trifle

Chocolate Truffle
Cheesecake

Christmas Crinkles
(page 133)

Serves 12

Christmas Crinkles, page 133;
Strawberry Holiday Trifle,
page 42; and Chocolate
Truffle Cheesecake, page 43

Strawberry Holiday Trifle

4 pts. strawberries, rinsed and
   hulled
3 T. sugar
Custard
¾ c. sliced almonds, divided
Sponge Cake, cut into one-inch
   cubes

¾ c. strawberry wine
Whipped topping
Garnish: one whole strawberry,
   sliced

Coarsely chop enough berries to measure 4 cups. Place in a bowl and stir in sugar; set aside. Spoon one cup Custard on bottom of a 12-cup trifle bowl. Sprinkle with ¼ cup almonds. Layer ½ of cake cubes over Custard; brush cake with ½ of wine. Spoon 2 cups berries over cake layer; top with one cup Custard. Repeat layers; top with remaining Custard. Cover and chill. Top with whipped topping; sprinkle with remaining almonds. Garnish, if desired. Makes 15 servings.

Custard

⅔ c. sugar
2 T. cornstarch
¼ t. salt
2 c. milk

4 egg yolks, lightly beaten
2 T. butter or margarine
1½ t. vanilla extract
1 c. whipping cream, whipped

Whisk together sugar, cornstarch, salt and milk in a saucepan. Cook over medium heat, stirring constantly, until thickened and bubbly. Stir about ¼ of hot mixture into egg yolks; add to remaining hot mixture, stirring constantly. Cook over medium heat, stirring constantly, 2 minutes. Remove from heat; add butter and vanilla, stirring until butter melts. Cover with plastic wrap, gently pressing it onto surface; chill at least 2 hours. Fold whipped cream into custard mixture. Makes 3½ cups.

Sponge Cake

2 eggs
1 c. sugar
1 c. all-purpose flour
1 t. baking powder

¼ t. salt
½ c. milk
2 T. butter or margarine
1 t. vanilla extract

Beat eggs at high speed with an electric mixer 3 minutes or until thick and pale. Gradually add sugar; beat 4 minutes. Combine flour, baking powder and salt; gradually fold into batter.
Combine milk and butter in a saucepan; cook over low heat until butter melts. Gradually stir milk mixture and vanilla into batter. Pour into 2 greased and floured 8" round cake pans.
Bake at 350 degrees for 16 minutes or until a toothpick inserted in center comes clean. Cool on wire racks 10 minutes. Remove from pans; cool completely on wire racks. Makes 2 (8-inch) cake layers.

Christmas Memories

"Christmas in our family is the best time to bake all those wonderful recipes that have been passed down from generation to generation or even from friend to friend. Sometimes the aromas bring back the most wonderful memories and hopefully create more for those new little ones around us."

–Rosalie Colby
Hiram, ME

Chocolate Truffle Cheesecake

1½ c. crushed cream-filled
   chocolate sandwich cookies
   (21 cookies)
¼ c. butter or margarine, melted
4 (8-oz.) pkgs. cream cheese,
   softened and divided
1½ c. sugar, divided
3 eggs
8-oz. container sour cream

2 t. vanilla extract, divided
1 c. semi-sweet chocolate chips,
   melted
⅓ c. seedless raspberry preserves
16-oz. container sour cream
½ c. semi-sweet chocolate chips
¼ c. whipping cream
Garnishes: whipped cream, fresh
   raspberries, mint sprigs

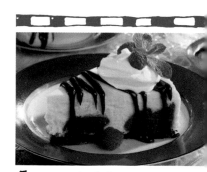

For ease, look for packaged crushed sandwich cookies in the cake mix section of your local supermarket.

   Combine cookie crumbs and butter in a bowl. Firmly press mixture in bottom of a 10" springform pan. Bake at 400 degrees for 8 minutes; cool in pan on a wire rack.

   Beat 3 packages cream cheese at medium speed with an electric mixer until creamy. Gradually add 1¼ cups sugar, beating well. Add eggs, one at a time, beating after each addition. Stir in an 8-ounce container sour cream and one teaspoon vanilla.

   Combine remaining package cream cheese, one cup melted chocolate chips and preserves in a bowl; stir well. Spoon ⅔ of vanilla batter into prepared crust. Drop chocolate mixture by rounded tablespoonfuls over batter; pour remaining batter over chocolate mixture. Bake at 325 degrees for 1 hour and 20 minutes or until almost set. (Cheesecake will rise above pan.) Increase oven temperature to 375 degrees.

   Combine a 16-ounce container sour cream, remaining ¼ cup sugar and remaining one teaspoon vanilla; spread over cheesecake. Bake 5 minutes. Cool in pan on a wire rack. Cover and chill 8 hours.

   To serve, remove sides of pan; slice cheesecake. Combine ½ cup chocolate chips and whipping cream in a saucepan; cook and stir over low heat until chocolate melts. Drizzle over slices. Garnish, if desired. Makes 12 servings.

Cookie Swap

Chess Brownies, page 46; Nutcracker Cookies, page 48; Mom Ford's Chocolate Chip Cookies, page 47; and Chocolate-Praline Truffles, page 48

Everyone benefits from a cookie swap… visiting with friends, nibbling on the treats and sharing the variety of goodies! To plan your own swap, ask each guest to make a dozen cookies for each person invited, plus extra to share at the party. And don't forget to bring the recipe! Check out our sampling of treats and try them at your own party…enjoy!

Menu

Chess Brownies

Millionaires

Mom Ford's Chocolate Chip Cookies

Nutcracker Cookies

Chocolate-Praline Truffles

Eggnog Cookies

Christmas Memories

"Mom and I started a tradition of spending one day together, usually the week before Christmas, to bake batches of cookies. Our day started by reading through volumes of cookie books and magazines to find new and exciting cookies to make. Then we'd don our special holiday aprons, drink lots of tea, listen to Christmas music and bake away! When the last batch was out of the oven and the last cookie frosted, Dad was invited into the kitchen to sample and 'ooh and ahh' over the day's accomplishments.

I keep these wonderful memories alive by decorating a small tree I keep on a pie pantry in my kitchen. On it I've hung my favorite cookie cutters from my mom's collection, along with a favorite poem glued inside a red heart cookie cutter."

–Melanie Elmore
Schenectady, NY

Chess Brownies

A box of cake mix makes quick work of these blond brownies loaded with pecans and topped with a soft cream cheese layer.

1 c. chopped pecans	18¼-oz. pkg. yellow cake mix
½ c. butter or margarine, melted	8-oz. pkg. cream cheese, softened
3 eggs	16-oz. pkg. powdered sugar

Stir together pecans, butter, one egg and cake mix until well blended; press in bottom of a lightly greased 13"x9" pan. Set aside.

Combine remaining 2 eggs, cream cheese and powdered sugar in a large mixing bowl; beat at medium speed with an electric mixer until smooth. Pour cream cheese mixture over cake mix layer.

Bake at 325 degrees for 40 minutes or until cheese mixture is set. Cool completely in pan on a wire rack. Cut into squares. Makes 15 brownies.

Millionaires

14-oz. pkg. caramels, unwrapped	2 c. chopped pecans
2 T. milk	2 c. semi-sweet chocolate chips

Combine caramels and milk in a heavy saucepan; cook over low heat until smooth, stirring often. Stir in pecans and drop by teaspoonfuls onto buttered baking sheets. Let stand until firm.

Microwave chocolate in a one-quart microwave-safe bowl on high power (100%) one minute or until melted, stirring once.

Dip candies into melted chocolate, allowing excess to drip; place on buttered baking sheets. Let stand until firm. Makes 34 candies.

Mom Ford's Chocolate Chip Cookies

½ c. shortening
⅓ c. sugar
⅓ c. brown sugar, packed
1 egg
½ t. vanilla extract

1 c. all-purpose flour
½ t. baking soda
¼ t. salt
1 c. semi-sweet chocolate chips
½ c. chopped pecans

Beat shortening at medium speed with an electric mixer until fluffy. Gradually add sugars, beating mixture well. Add egg and vanilla, beating until blended.

Stir together flour, soda and salt; add to shortening mixture, mixing well. Stir in chocolate chips and pecans.

Drop dough by tablespoonfuls onto ungreased baking sheets. Bake at 350 degrees for 10 to 12 minutes. Transfer to wire racks to cool. Makes 2 dozen.

Nutcracker Cookies

(pictured on page 45)

2 c. butter or margarine, softened	¼ t. salt
1 c. sugar	2 t. vanilla extract
3 egg yolks	1 t. almond extract
4¼ c. all-purpose flour	Powdered Sugar Paints
¼ t. baking powder	

Beat butter at medium speed with an electric mixer until creamy; gradually add sugar, beating well. Add egg yolks, one at a time, beating until blended after each addition.

Stir together flour, baking powder and salt; gradually add to butter mixture, beating at low speed until blended after each addition. Stir in flavorings. Divide dough in half; wrap each portion in plastic wrap. Chill at least 4 hours.

Roll one portion of dough at a time to ¼-inch thickness on a lightly floured surface. Cut with a 7-inch toy soldier cutter and place 2 inches apart on lightly greased baking sheets.

Bake at 350 degrees for 15 minutes or until edges are golden. Cool on baking sheets on wire racks 3 minutes; then remove cookies to wire racks to cool completely.

Decorate with Powdered Sugar Paints, using a small spatula or paintbrush. Makes 1½ dozen.

Powdered Sugar Paints

3 c. sifted powdered sugar	1 t. vanilla extract
2 T. light corn syrup	Assorted liquid food coloring
2 to 3 T. milk	

Stir together sugar and corn syrup; stir in milk and vanilla to desired spreading consistency. Divide into several small bowls; stir drops of a different food coloring into each bowl. Makes about 3 cups.

Chocolate-Praline Truffles

(pictured on page 45)

1½ c. chopped pecans	¼ c. whipping cream
¼ c. brown sugar, packed	3 T. butter, cut into pieces
2 T. whipping cream	2 T. almond liqueur
3 (4-oz.) semi-sweet chocolate bars, broken into pieces	

Stir together pecans, brown sugar and 2 tablespoons whipping cream; spread in a lightly buttered 9" round cake pan.

Bake at 350 degrees for 20 minutes or until coating appears slightly crystallized, stirring once. Remove from oven; stir and cool.

Microwave chocolate and ¼ cup whipping cream in a 2-quart microwave-safe bowl on medium power (50%) 3½ minutes. Whisk until chocolate melts and mixture is smooth. (If chocolate doesn't melt completely, microwave and whisk at 15 second intervals until melted.) Whisk in butter and liqueur; let stand 20 minutes.

Beat mixture at medium speed with an electric mixer 4 minutes or until mixture forms soft peaks. (Do not overbeat mixture.) Cover and chill at least 4 hours.

Shape mixture into one-inch balls; roll in pecans. Cover and chill up to one week or freeze up to one month. Makes about 2 dozen.

White Chocolate-Praline Truffles: Substitute 3 (4-ounce) white chocolate bars for semi-sweet chocolate bars and almonds for pecans.

Chocolate-Marble Truffles: Prepare one recipe each of mixture for Chocolate-Praline Truffles and White Chocolate-Praline Truffles. Spoon both mixtures into a 13"x9" pan; swirl with a knife. Chill and shape as directed; roll in chocolate sandwich cookie crumbs, omitting pecan mixture.

Eggnog Cookies

1 c. butter, softened
2 c. sugar
5½ c. all-purpose flour
1 t. baking soda
½ t. nutmeg

1 c. eggnog
1 egg white, lightly beaten
  (optional)
1 T. water (optional)
Colored sugar crystals

Beat butter at medium speed with an electric mixer until creamy; gradually add 2 cups sugar, beating well.

Combine flour, soda and nutmeg; add to butter mixture alternately with eggnog, beginning and ending with flour mixture. Cover and chill dough at least one hour.

Divide dough in half. Work with one portion of dough at a time, storing remainder in refrigerator. Roll each portion of dough to ⅛-inch thickness on a lightly floured surface. Cut with a 4-inch cookie cutter; place on lightly greased baking sheets.

If desired, combine egg white and water in a small bowl; brush cookies with egg white mixture. Sprinkle with colored sugar. Bake at 375 degrees for 8 to 10 minutes or until lightly browned. Cool slightly on baking sheets; remove to wire racks and let cool completely. Makes 4½ dozen.

Brushing the cookie dough with an egg white mixture helps to keep the sugar crystals in place.

Clockwise from top left:
Gingerbread Trifle, page 132;
Homestyle Green Beans,
page 105; Baked Maple Ham,
page 68; Roasted Sweet
Potato Salad, page 102

Our Favorite Christmas Recipes

Let this collection of delicious recipes win raves at all your special occasions this Christmas season. Each recipe was hand-selected for the best flavor & holiday appeal.

Tree-Trimming Treats

Page 60

Let the party begin with these

tantalizing appetizers and beverages.

You'll find just the right selection

to make your special gathering

merry & bright!

Hot Candy Cane Nog,
page 55

Hot Buttered Rum

1 qt. vanilla ice cream, softened
16-oz. pkg. brown sugar
16-oz. pkg. powdered sugar
2 c. butter or margarine, softened
2 t. cinnamon
1 to 2 t. nutmeg
Light rum (optional)

Combine ice cream, brown sugar, powdered sugar, butter, cinnamon and nutmeg in a large bowl. Beat at medium speed with an electric mixer until well blended. Spoon mixture into a 2-quart container; freeze.

To serve, thaw slightly. For each serving, place ¼ cup ice cream mixture and, if desired, a jigger of rum (2 to 4 tablespoons) in a large mug; fill with boiling water and stir well. Makes about 25 servings.

Hot Percolator Punch

★ ★ ★

Here's a classic punch that sends an inviting cinnamon aroma throughout your house as it perks. This is an easy recipe to double if you have a large percolator and a big crowd to serve.

3 c. unsweetened pineapple juice
3 c. cranberry-apple juice drink
1 c. water
⅓ c. light brown sugar
2 lemon slices
2 (4-inch) cinnamon sticks, broken
1½ t. whole cloves
Cinnamon sticks (optional)

Pour juices and water into a percolator. Place brown sugar, lemon slices, cinnamon sticks and cloves in percolator basket. Perk through complete cycle of electric percolator. Serve with additional cinnamon sticks, if desired. Makes 7 cups.

Little Holiday Touches

• Keep a basket or wooden bowl by the front door filled with home-made ornaments. Give them to family & friends when they head home after your party. These little gifts are also a nice surprise for neighbors, teachers or people who deliver the mail or newspaper.

• A handy way to serve cold drinks at a party is to line your favorite basket with plastic and fill it with crushed ice. This will keep miniature bottles of soft drinks or bottled water cold and at your guests' fingertips.

• Wax seal the envelopes of your Christmas cards or party invitations. Card and gift shops carry an assortment of designs that look festive with red, green or gold wax.

–Melissa Shride
Greenville, SC

Hot Candy Cane Nog

(pictured on page 53)

★ ★ ★

6 c. milk
8 (1.5-oz.) chocolate-covered
  peppermint patties
1 c. white crème de cacao
  (optional)

French vanilla or chocolate ice
  cream
6 peppermint sticks

    Pour milk into a small saucepan. Cook over medium heat, stirring constantly, 5 minutes or until hot but not boiling (about 180 degrees). Pour 2 cups hot milk into blender; add peppermint patties. Cover and process on low speed until smooth. Add peppermint mixture to remaining milk in saucepan. Add crème de cacao, if desired. Cook until heated through (about 140 degrees). Pour into mugs. Top with a scoop of ice cream and a peppermint stick. Makes 6 servings.

Melt chocolate-peppermint candies in warm milk, top with a generous scoop of ice cream and what do you have? The ultimate holiday treat that will satisfy all your holiday guests. Garnish with peppermint sticks for a festive touch and for an extra bit of cool peppermint flavor.

Spiced Red Zinger Cider

★

1 qt. water
6 Red Zinger tea bags
24 whole cloves
1 orange
Cheesecloth
24 whole allspice

3 (3-inch) cinnamon sticks, broken
5 c. apple cider
5 c. cranberry juice drink
½ c. sugar
1½ c. dark rum (optional)
Cinnamon sticks (optional)

    Bring water to a boil; add tea bags. Remove from heat; cover and steep 5 minutes. Remove and discard tea bags.
    Insert cloves into skin of orange. Cut a 6-inch square of cheesecloth; place allspice and broken cinnamon sticks in center and tie with string.
    Combine tea, orange, spice bag, cider, cranberry juice and sugar in a Dutch oven; bring to a boil. Cover, reduce heat and simmer one hour. Remove from heat; cool to room temperature. Remove and discard orange and spice bag. (At this point, you can refrigerate mixture in a nonmetal airtight container up to 3 days.)
    To serve, combine cider mixture and, if desired, rum in Dutch oven; cook over low heat until hot, stirring occasionally. Ladle cider into mugs; serve warm with cinnamon-stick stirrers, if desired. Makes 14 cups.

Serve spiced pecans on page 57 for guests to munch on while they sip this zesty cider.

Mocha Punch with Chocolate-Peppermint Bundt® Cake (page 128)

Mocha Punch

For a non-alcoholic version, substitute amaretto-flavored non-dairy liquid creamer for Kahlúa or increase coffee to 5 cups.

1 qt. chocolate milk
4 c. strong brewed coffee, chilled
1 c. Kahlúa or other coffee-flavored liqueur
14-oz. can sweetened condensed milk

1 qt. chocolate ice cream
1 qt. coffee ice cream
Semi-sweet chocolate shavings

Combine chocolate milk, coffee, liqueur and condensed milk in a large pitcher. Cover and chill. Pour chilled mixture into a large punch bowl. Scoop chocolate and coffee ice creams into punch; stir gently. Sprinkle with chocolate shavings. Makes 18 cups.

Sparkling Cinnamon Punch

1 c. water
½ c. sugar
½ c. red cinnamon candies
2 (2-ltr.) bottles raspberry ginger
  ale or regular ginger ale, chilled

46-oz. can apple juice or apple
  cider, chilled

Combine first 3 ingredients in a small saucepan; bring to a boil. Reduce heat and simmer, uncovered, 5 minutes or until candies melt, stirring occasionally. Cool completely.

Combine cinnamon mixture, ginger ale and apple juice in a large punch bowl; stir well. Makes 25 cups.

Spiced Pecans

1 c. sugar
2 t. cinnamon
1 t. salt
½ t. nutmeg

¼ t. ground cloves
¼ c. water
3 c. pecan halves, toasted

Combine sugar, cinnamon, salt, nutmeg, cloves and water in a small saucepan. Cook over medium-low heat, stirring constantly, until sugar dissolves. Cook 9 more minutes on medium-low or until a candy thermometer registers 236 degrees (soft-ball stage). Do not stir. Place pecans in a large bowl; pour hot mixture over pecans. Stir until they start to lose their gloss.

Spread pecans on wax paper and separate quickly with a fork. Cool completely. Store in an airtight container. Makes 3 cups.

Herb-Marinated Cheese

½ c. olive oil
¼ c. herbal vinegar
3 to 4 cloves garlic, pressed
1 T. fresh parsley, chopped
½ t. peppercorns

¼ t. fennel seed
4- to 6-oz. sharp Cheddar cheese, cubed
4- to 6-oz. provolone cheese, cubed
1 bay leaf

Whisk together first 6 ingredients in a medium bowl. Add cubed cheese and bay leaf; cover tightly. Refrigerate and marinate for one to 4 days, stirring each day. Remove cheese from bowl with slotted spoon; serve with sourdough bread. Makes 4 servings.

Salmon Party Log

8-oz. pkg. cream cheese, softened
16-oz. can salmon, bone and skin removed
1 T. lemon juice
2 t. grated onion

1 t. prepared horseradish
¼ t. salt
¼ t. Worcestershire sauce
½ c. chopped pecans
3 T. fresh parsley, chopped

Beat cream cheese at medium speed with an electric mixer until creamy. Add salmon and next 5 ingredients. Shape into 2 (6-inch) logs. Place pecans and parsley on wax paper; roll logs in mixture until coated. Cover and chill at least 2 hours. Serve with crackers. Makes 2 (6-inch) logs.

Florentine Artichoke Dip

10-oz. pkg. frozen chopped
  spinach, thawed
2 (6½-oz.) jars marinated
  artichoke hearts, drained and
  chopped
1½ (8-oz.) pkgs. cream cheese,
  softened
1 c. freshly shredded Parmesan
  cheese

½ c. mayonnaise
3 large cloves garlic, pressed
2 T. lemon juice
1½ c. freshly prepared French
  bread crumbs
2 T. butter or margarine, melted

Drain spinach; press between layers of paper towels to remove excess moisture.

Combine spinach, artichoke hearts and next 5 ingredients in a bowl, stirring well. Spoon into a lightly greased 11"x7" baking dish. Combine bread crumbs and butter; sprinkle over spinach mixture.

Bake, uncovered, at 375 degrees for 25 minutes. Serve with assorted crackers, bagel chips or bread sticks. Makes 4 cups.

Sausage Stars

25-count pkg. won ton wrappers
1 lb. sausage, cooked and
  crumbled
1½ c. grated sharp Cheddar cheese

1½ c. grated Monterey Jack cheese
1 c. ranch-style salad dressing
2¼-oz. can sliced black olives
½ c. chopped red pepper

"This is one of my favorite appetizers. To save time, I make the filling ahead and before serving, fill the wrappers and bake!"
—Geri Peterson
Pleasanton, CA

Press one won ton wrapper in each cup of a muffin tin; bake at 350 degrees for 5 minutes. Remove won tons and place on a baking sheet. Repeat with remaining won tons; set aside.

Combine sausage and remaining 5 ingredients and evenly fill baked wrappers. Bake 5 more minutes or until bubbly. Makes 25 appetizers.

Black Bean Tartlets

This Southwestern appetizer sports a festive red and green filling with spicy flavor.

1¼ c. all-purpose flour
¾ c. yellow cornmeal
½ c. shredded Monterey Jack cheese with peppers
1 t. salt
1 t. cumin
1 t. chili powder
½ t. garlic powder

½ t. ground red pepper
½ c. cold butter or margarine, cut into pieces
1 egg, lightly beaten
2 T. ice water
Black Bean Salsa
Garnishes: sour cream, fresh cilantro

Process first 8 ingredients in a food processor until blended. Add butter and process until mixture is crumbly. Add egg and ice water; process just until mixture forms a ball.

Divide dough in half; shape each half of dough into 16 (one-inch) balls. Press balls into lightly greased miniature (1¾") muffin pans, pressing evenly into bottom and up sides.

Bake tartlet shells at 450 degrees for 8 minutes or until lightly browned. Cool in pans 10 minutes; remove shells to wire racks and cool completely.

When ready to serve, spoon one tablespoon Black Bean Salsa into each tartlet shell; garnish, if desired. Serve at room temperature. Makes 32 appetizers.

Black Bean Salsa

15-oz. can black beans, drained
2 canned chipotle chilies in adobo sauce, minced
3 green onions, chopped
½ c. finely chopped yellow pepper

1 plum tomato, finely chopped
1 T. chopped fresh cilantro
2 T. fresh lime juice
1 T. olive oil
½ t. salt

Combine all ingredients in a bowl, tossing well. Cover and chill at least one hour. Makes 2¼ cups.

Roasted Red Pepper Bruschetta

12-oz. jar roasted red peppers,
  drained well and finely chopped
½ c. finely chopped plum tomato
¼ c. finely chopped red onion
2 T. balsamic vinegar
2 T. olive oil
½ t. salt

½ t. freshly ground pepper
⅛ t. sugar
1 baguette, cut into 28 slices
¼ c. olive oil
Salt and black pepper
½ c. crumbled garlic and herb-
  flavored feta cheese

Combine first 3 ingredients in a bowl. Combine vinegar, 2 tablespoons olive oil, salt, pepper and sugar; pour over roasted pepper mixture and toss well. Cover and chill up to a day.

When ready to serve, arrange baguette slices on a large ungreased baking sheet. Brush or drizzle slices with ¼ cup olive oil. Sprinkle with salt and pepper. Bake at 400 degrees for 4 minutes or until barely toasted. Spoon about one tablespoon pepper mixture onto each baguette slice; top each with crumbled cheese. Broil 5½ inches from heat 3 minutes or until bubbly and barely browned. Serve warm. Makes 28 appetizers.

We topped these toasts with a sweet-tangy roasted red pepper mix and feta cheese. The combination makes a pretty hors d'oeuvre for a holiday party.

Yuletide Crab Puffs

1 lb. fresh lump crabmeat, drained
  and flaked
1½ c. mayonnaise
⅔ c. chopped celery
½ c. chopped onion
4 eggs, hard-boiled, peeled and
  chopped
1 T. fresh parsley, minced

2 T. chili sauce
½ t. salt
½ t. pepper
1 c. boiling water
½ c. butter or margarine, cut into
  pieces
1 c. all-purpose flour
4 eggs, lightly beaten

Combine first 9 ingredients. Cover and chill filling.

Combine boiling water and butter in a medium bowl; stir until butter melts. Add flour and stir vigorously until mixture leaves sides of pan and forms a smooth ball. Let mixture cool 2 minutes. Add eggs, beating vigorously with a wooden spoon until dough is smooth. Drop by teaspoonfuls onto an ungreased baking sheet.

Bake at 400 degrees for 25 minutes or until puffed and golden; remove puffs from pan and cool on a wire rack. Cut top off each puff, using a serrated knife. Fill each puff with a heaping tablespoon of filling and replace top. Makes 2 dozen.

Note: *Puffs may appear done before baking time is completed, but they may fall if they're taken out of the oven too soon.*

These savory puffs can be made ahead of time and frozen or stored in an airtight container until ready to fill. The filling can be made several hours in advance and spooned into the puffs just before serving.

Memorable Main Dishes

Page 69

Satisfy eager appetites
with any one of these delectable
entrées. You'll find a variety of
main dishes that will feed the
smallest to largest crowds on
your holiday guest list.

Baked Maple Ham,
page 68

Juicy Prime Rib

¼ c. ground red pepper
2 T. salt
2 T. ground white pepper
1½ t. garlic powder

1½ t. dried thyme
1 t. onion powder
8- to 10-lb. boneless beef rib-eye
   roast

Combine first 6 ingredients; lightly press on top and sides of roast.

Place roast, fat side up, in a shallow roasting pan; insert a meat thermometer into the thickest part of roast, making sure it does not touch fat.

Bake, uncovered, at 425 degrees for 10 minutes. Reduce temperature to 325 degrees; bake 2 hours and 40 minutes or until thermometer registers 145 degrees (medium-rare) or 160 degrees (medium).

Remove roast to a serving platter. Let stand 15 minutes before carving. Makes 12 to 16 servings.

Winter's Night Pot Roast

2 T. vegetable oil
2½- to 3-lb. boneless chuck roast
1 t. sugar
2 t. salt, divided
1 t. pepper
3 T. steak sauce
1 t. dried thyme

½ t. dried basil
3 onions, peeled and quartered
4 c. water
6 potatoes, peeled and quartered
4 carrots, peeled and sliced
5 T. all-purpose flour

Heat oil in a Dutch oven over high heat. Add roast and brown on all sides; sprinkle with sugar, 1½ teaspoons salt, and pepper. Stir in steak sauce, thyme and basil. Add onion and water. Bring to a boil, reduce heat, and simmer, covered, 2 hours. Add potatoes and carrots and continue to cook one more hour or until vegetables are tender.

Remove roast and vegetables with a slotted spoon. Cover and keep warm. Reserve 4 cups broth in Dutch oven. Combine flour and ½ cup cooled broth, stirring until smooth. Whisk into remaining 3½ cups broth in Dutch oven over medium-high heat, stirring constantly. Bring to a boil. Boil 5 minutes or until thickened. Add remaining ½ teaspoon salt. Serve gravy with pot roast and vegetables. Makes 6 to 8 servings.

Beef Tenderloin

2 T. vegetable oil
3-lb. beef tenderloin, trimmed
2 T. sliced green onion
1½ c. beef broth
¼ c. cold butter or margarine,
  cut into pieces

2 T. pine nuts, toasted
2 T. sliced almonds, toasted
2 T. chopped walnuts, toasted
2 oz. crumbled blue cheese

Pour oil into a large skillet; place over medium-high heat until hot. Place tenderloin in skillet and brown on all sides.

Place tenderloin on a rack in a shallow roasting pan. Bake at 450 degrees for 30 to 35 minutes or until a meat thermometer inserted in thickest part of meat registers 145 degrees (medium-rare) or 160 degrees (medium).

Meanwhile, add green onion and broth to pan drippings. Cook over medium-high heat, stirring constantly, until mixture comes to a boil (about 5 minutes). Remove from heat; whisk in butter until melted. Stir in pine nuts.

Place tenderloin on a serving platter; sprinkle with almonds, walnuts and blue cheese. Serve with warm sauce. Makes 8 to 10 servings.

Filet Mignon with Mushrooms

1 T. vegetable oil
8-oz. pkg. sliced mushrooms
4 cloves garlic, minced
4 (6-oz.) beef tenderloin filets

½ t. salt
½ t. pepper
½ t. garlic powder
⅓ c. marsala wine or beef broth

Pour oil into a large skillet; place over medium-high heat until hot. Add mushrooms and garlic; cook 5 minutes or until liquid evaporates, stirring frequently. Remove from heat.

Meanwhile, sprinkle each filet with salt, pepper and garlic powder. Place filets on a lightly greased rack in a broiler pan; broil 3 inches from heat 5 to 6 minutes on each side or to desired degree of doneness.

Add wine to mushroom mixture and bring to a boil; cook 2 minutes or until wine is almost absorbed. Place each filet on a serving plate and top with mushroom mixture. Makes 4 servings.

Mustard-Crusted Pork Roast & Browned Potatoes

★ ★ ★

Rosemary potatoes roast alongside this mustardy pork. Peeling the potatoes adds to the presentation.

4- to 5-lb. boneless pork loin
  roast
¼ t. salt
¼ t. pepper
½ c. coarse-grained mustard
8 cloves garlic, minced
3 T. olive oil
3 T. balsamic vinegar

2 T. chopped fresh rosemary
2 lbs. new potatoes
2 T. olive oil
1 T. chopped fresh rosemary
½ t. salt
½ t. pepper
Garnish: fresh rosemary sprigs

Place pork in a greased roasting pan. Rub with ¼ teaspoon each salt and pepper. Combine mustard and next 4 ingredients in a small bowl; spread evenly over pork.

Peel a crosswise strip around each potato with a vegetable peeler, if desired. Cut each potato in half lengthwise. Toss potatoes with 2 table-spoons oil, one tablespoon chopped rosemary, ½ teaspoon salt and ½ tea-spoon pepper. Add to roasting pan around pork. Insert a meat thermometer into thickest part of roast.

Bake at 375 degrees for one hour to 1¼ hours or until thermometer regis-ters 160 degrees. Let stand 10 minutes. Transfer roast to a serving platter. Surround pork with potatoes. Garnish, if desired. Makes 8 to 10 servings.

Pork & Raspberry Sauce

3- to 4-lb. boneless pork loin
   roast
1 t. salt

1 t. pepper
1 t. sage
Raspberry Sauce

Sprinkle roast with salt, pepper and sage. Place roast on a rack in a shallow roasting pan. Bake at 325 degrees for 1½ to 2 hours or until a meat thermometer registers 160 degrees. Place roast on a platter and serve with Raspberry Sauce. Makes 10 to 12 servings.

Raspberry Sauce

12-oz. frozen raspberries, thawed
3 c. sugar
½ c. white vinegar
½ t. ground cloves
½ t. ground ginger

½ t. nutmeg
½ c. cornstarch
2 T. lemon juice
2 T. butter or margarine, melted
6 to 8 drops red food coloring

Drain raspberries, reserving juice. Add water to juice, if necessary, to make 1½ cups. Combine 1 cup raspberry liquid, sugar, vinegar, cloves, ginger and nutmeg in a saucepan. Bring to a boil; reduce heat and simmer, uncovered, 10 minutes. Whisk together cornstarch and remaining ½ cup raspberry liquid; add to saucepan. Cook over medium heat, stirring constantly, one minute or until thickened. Stir in raspberries, lemon juice, butter and food coloring. Makes 10 to 12 servings.

Memorable Entertaining Tips

•Plan menus with recipes that can be made early and save easy tasks for the day of your party. Then you'll have plenty of time for last minute touches without feeling rushed.

•Group seasonal fruits and vegetables down the center of the table for a simple holiday centerpiece.

•Go ahead and use your fine china and favorite serving pieces...it'll make your guests feel extra special.

•Fill your house with candles...especially chunky pillars so you don't have to worry as much about wax drippings. Your entire house will feel warm and smell fragrant, setting a welcoming tone to your party. Place candles in rooms where your guests will gather and also tuck them in bedrooms and bathrooms.

•When friends come for dinner, give them small favors as a remembrance of the evening. Use gifts that can work as napkin rings or placecards such as napkins tied with oversized jingle bells or miniature ornaments personalized with guests' names.

Pork Tenderloins with Cranberry Chutney

Cinnamon-cranberry chutney makes a tangy topping for grilled tenderloins. We used a Rome Beauty apple in our chutney.

2 (¾-lb.) pork tenderloins, trimmed
¼ c. soy sauce
2 T. brown sugar

3 T. honey
½ t. ground ginger
Cranberry Chutney

Place tenderloins in a large heavy-duty, plastic zipping bag. Combine soy sauce, brown sugar, honey and ginger; pour over tenderloins. Seal bag and marinate in refrigerator 8 hours, turning bag occasionally. Remove tenderloins from marinade, reserving marinade. Place marinade in a small saucepan; bring to a boil. Remove from heat; set aside.

Grill tenderloins, covered, over medium-high heat (350 degrees to 400 degrees) 20 to 25 minutes or until a meat thermometer inserted into thickest part of tenderloin registers 160 degrees, turning occasionally and basting with reserved marinade. Let tenderloins stand 10 minutes before slicing. Serve with Cranberry Chutney. Makes 6 servings.

Cranberry Chutney

4 c. fresh cranberries
2 c. sugar
1 c. chopped cooking apple
½ c. raisins
¼ c. chopped onion

¼ c. chopped walnuts
¼ c. orange juice
1 T. white vinegar
½ t. cinnamon
½ t. ground ginger

Combine all ingredients in a saucepan; bring to a boil. Cover, reduce heat, and simmer 45 minutes, stirring occasionally. Cover and chill until ready to serve. Makes 3 cups.

Baked Maple Ham

(pictured on page 63)

Reheating a fully-cooked ham to 140 degrees is recommended to bring out the most flavor. Store leftover ham tightly wrapped in aluminum foil in the refrigerator.

8- to 9-lb. smoked fully cooked
   ham shank
Whole cloves
1¼ c. brown sugar, packed
½ c. maple syrup

Garnishes: apple slices, orange slices, fresh flat-leaf parsley sprigs

Slice skin from ham. Score top of ham in a diamond pattern, making cuts ⅛-inch deep. Stud with whole cloves. Place ham, fat side up, on a rack in a shallow roasting pan. Insert a meat thermometer into center of ham, making sure it does not touch bone or fat. Bake at 325 degrees for 2 to 2½ hours or until meat thermometer registers 135 degrees.

Combine brown sugar and maple syrup in a small bowl; stir well. Brush brown sugar mixture over ham. Bake 20 to 30 more minutes or until thermometer registers 140 degrees. Remove from oven and let stand 10 minutes before slicing. Garnish, if desired. Makes 16 servings.

Garlic White Lasagna

1½ lbs. hot Italian sausage
  (in casings)
4 large cloves garlic, chopped
1 medium onion, chopped
12-oz. jar roasted red pepper,
  drained and chopped
½ c. white wine
10-oz. pkg. frozen chopped spinach
15-oz. container ricotta cheese
½ t. salt

½ t. pepper
1 egg, lightly beaten
2 (16-oz.) jars creamy Alfredo
  sauce
12 lasagna noodles, uncooked
2 (6-oz.) pkgs. sliced mozzarella
  cheese
1 c. grated or finely shredded
  refrigerated Parmesan cheese

Easy Lasagna? No problem. We use ready-made Alfredo sauce and skip the boiling water…the uncooked noodles soften in the creamy sauce and fully cook as the lasagna bakes. Hot Italian sausage and fresh garlic punch up the flavor.

Remove and discard sausage casings. Brown sausage in a large skillet over medium heat, using a wooden spoon to crumble sausage as it cooks.

Drain sausage, reserving one tablespoon drippings in skillet. Cook garlic and onion in reserved drippings over medium-high heat until onion is tender. Stir in sausage, chopped red pepper and wine. Bring to a boil; reduce heat and simmer, uncovered, 5 minutes or until most of liquid has evaporated.

Meanwhile, cook spinach according to package directions; drain and squeeze between paper towels to remove excess liquid. Combine spinach, ricotta cheese and next 3 ingredients; stir well.

Spread one cup Alfredo sauce in a greased 13"x9" baking dish. Top with 4 uncooked noodles. Top with half of spinach mixture and half of sausage mixture. Place 4 slices mozzarella over sausage mixture. Repeat layers.

Top with remaining 4 noodles and mozzarella slices. Spread remaining Alfredo sauce over mozzarella cheese. Sprinkle with Parmesan cheese (If desired, cover and chill overnight. Let stand at room temperature 30 minutes before baking.)

Cover and bake at 350 degrees for one hour, uncovering during last 15 minutes of baking. Let stand 15 minutes before serving. Makes 8 servings.

Maple Roast Chicken & Veggies

1 winter squash, peeled and chopped
3 to 4 parsnips, peeled and chopped
2 stalks celery, chopped
2 carrots, chopped
1 onion, chopped
1 sweet potato, peeled and chopped

6- to 7-lb. whole chicken
2 T. butter or margarine, melted
½ t. salt
¼ t. pepper
½ t. dried rosemary
½ c. maple syrup

Spread vegetables evenly in a lightly greased roasting pan; place chicken on top. Brush chicken with butter; sprinkle with salt, pepper and rosemary. Place on lowest rack in oven and bake at 400 degrees for 1½ to 2 hours or until a meat thermometer inserted in thigh registers 180 degrees. Baste about every 10 minutes with maple syrup and pan drippings. Remove from oven and let stand 10 minutes before slicing. Makes 4 to 6 servings.

Roast Turkey & Gravy

8 slices of bacon, crisply cooked and crumbled
1 c. unsalted butter, softened
3 T. chopped fresh sage
Salt and pepper to taste
16-lb. turkey

3 c. chopped leeks, white and green parts
8 lg. fresh sage sprigs
3 bay leaves, crumbled
4½ c. canned chicken broth
Garnish: fresh sage and parsley

Combine bacon, butter, sage, and salt and pepper to taste in a medium bowl; set aside.

Remove giblets and neck from turkey; reserve for other uses. Rinse turkey with cold water; pat dry. Sprinkle body cavity with additional salt and pepper. Place leeks, sage sprigs and bay leaves in cavity. Place turkey on a greased rack in a large roasting pan. Lift wingtips up and over back and tuck under bird.

Loosen skin from turkey breast without totally detaching skin. Spread ⅓ cup sage butter under skin; rub 2 tablespoons sage butter over outside of turkey. Set aside ⅓ cup sage butter for gravy; reserve remaining for basting.

Bake turkey at 350 degrees for 3 hours or until a meat thermometer inserted in meaty part of thigh registers 180 degrees, basting every 30 minutes with ⅓ cup broth and sage butter.

Transfer turkey to a platter and let stand 30 minutes before slicing. Garnish, if desired.

To prepare gravy, pour pan drippings into a large glass measuring cup; spoon off fat and discard. Pour juices into a saucepan; add 2 cups broth and bring to a boil. Boil until liquid is reduced to 2 cups. Whisk in reserved ⅓ cup sage butter and season to taste. Makes 12 to 14 servings.

Honey-Glazed Turkey Breast

¼ c. honey
1 T. Dijon mustard
1 T. Worcestershire sauce
1 T. butter or margarine, melted

3-lb. boneless turkey breast
1 T. vegetable oil
1 t. salt
½ t. pepper

"Just the right size for a family dinner."
—Adrienne Payne
Omaha, NE

Stir together first 4 ingredients; set aside.

Rinse turkey breast and pat dry with paper towels; brush with oil. Place in a shallow roasting pan. Sprinkle turkey breast with salt and pepper. Baste turkey breast with honey mixture.

Roast turkey breast at 325 degrees for 1 hour and 25 minutes or until thermometer registers 170 degrees. Baste with honey glaze during the last 25 minutes of baking. Transfer turkey to a platter and let stand 15 minutes before slicing. Makes 6 servings.

Cranberry-Orange Glazed Cornish Hens

2 Cornish hens (about 1¼ lbs. each)
2 T. butter or margarine, melted
1 t. salt
½ t. pepper
¼ c. whole-berry cranberry sauce

2 T. orange marmalade
1 T. lemon juice
1 t. dried, minced onion
1 t. cornstarch
½ c. mandarin orange sections, drained

When buying Cornish hens, look for the smallest birds you can find…they're the most tender and have the best flavor. Typically, one Cornish hen serves one person, but large or stuffed hens can be split to serve two.

Remove and discard giblets and neck from hens; rinse hens with cold water and pat dry. Coat inside and outside of hens with butter; sprinkle outside with salt and pepper. Place hens, breast side down, on an ungreased rack in a shallow roasting pan. Insert a meat thermometer into meatiest portion of thigh of one hen; cover loosely with aluminum foil.

Bake at 375 degrees for 30 minutes; uncover and bake one hour or until meat thermometer registers 180 degrees.

Meanwhile, combine cranberry sauce and next 4 ingredients in a small saucepan; bring to a boil. Reduce heat and simmer 2 minutes or until thickened and bubbly, stirring often. Stir in orange sections. Spoon mixture over hens during last 20 minutes of baking. Makes 2 to 4 servings.

Roast Duck with Cherry Sauce

Go beyond basic turkey this holiday season with this colorful, top-rated entrée.

5- to 6-lb. dressed duckling
1 small orange, quartered
2 sprigs fresh parsley
1 small onion, quartered
1 carrot, scraped and quartered
1 stalk celery, halved

½ t. salt
¼ t. pepper
Garnishes: fresh cherries, fresh
   flat-leaf parsley sprigs, orange
   slices
Cherry Sauce

Remove giblets and neck from duckling; reserve for another use. Rinse duckling thoroughly with cold water; pat dry with paper towels.

Rub one orange quarter over skin and inside cavity of duckling. Place remaining orange quarters, 2 parsley sprigs and next 3 ingredients in cavity of duckling; close cavity with skewers. Tie ends of legs together with string. Lift wingtips up and over back and tuck under duckling.

Sprinkle with salt and pepper. Place duckling on a greased rack in a shallow roasting pan, breast side up. Insert meat thermometer into meaty portion of thigh, making sure it does not touch bone.

Bake, uncovered, at 425 degrees for 45 minutes. Reduce oven temperature to 400 degrees; bake 35 minutes or until meat thermometer registers 180 degrees. Turn duckling often during baking for more even browning and crisping of skin, if desired. Transfer duckling to a serving platter; let stand 10 minutes before slicing. Garnish, if desired. Serve with Cherry Sauce. Makes 4 servings.

Cherry Sauce

16½-oz. can Bing cherries in heavy
   syrup, undrained
½ c. sugar
1½ T. cornstarch

¼ t. salt
2 T. red wine vinegar
2 T. lemon juice

Drain cherries, reserving ⅔ cup syrup; set aside. Combine sugar, cornstarch and salt in a small saucepan; gradually stir in reserved syrup. Cook over medium-high heat, stirring constantly, until thick and bubbly. Stir in cherries, vinegar and lemon juice; cook until heated. Makes 2 cups.

Seafood Casserole

2½ lbs. unpeeled, large fresh
   shrimp
½ c. butter or margarine
½ c. chopped green pepper
½ c. chopped onion
½ c. chopped celery
8-oz. pkg. sliced mushrooms
⅔ c. all-purpose flour
½ t. minced garlic
½ t. salt
¼ t. paprika

¼ t. ground red pepper
10¾-oz. can cream of shrimp soup
2 c. milk
1 lb. fresh lump crabmeat, drained
8-oz. can water chestnuts,
   drained
¼ c. butter or margarine, melted
1 c. freshly prepared bread crumbs
1 c. shredded sharp Cheddar
   cheese

Peel shrimp and devein, if desired; set aside.

Melt ½ cup butter in a large skillet over medium-high heat. Add green pepper, onion, celery and mushrooms; sauté 5 minutes or until tender. Stir in flour; cook one minute. Add garlic and next 3 ingredients. Whisk in soup and milk until smooth; cook one minute or until thickened.

Combine shrimp, crabmeat and water chestnuts in a large bowl. Pour sauce over seafood; stir well. Pour seafood mixture into a lightly greased 13"x9" baking dish.

Combine ¼ cup butter, bread crumbs and cheese in a small bowl; sprinkle evenly over casserole. Bake, uncovered, at 350 degrees for 30 minutes or until bubbly. Makes 8 to 10 servings.

Baked Jumbo Shrimp

2 lbs. unpeeled, jumbo fresh
   shrimp
¼ c. butter or margarine
2 T. fresh parsley, chopped

¼ c. fresh lemon juice
2 T. olive oil
2 T. vegetable oil

Christmas doesn't have to be the traditional turkey meal...especially for shrimp-lovers!

Peel shrimp and devein, if desired.

Melt butter in a 13"x9" baking dish at 450 degrees; heat until butter is foamy. Remove dish from oven. Add parsley, lemon juice, olive oil and vegetable oil; stir well. Add shrimp to butter mixture, turning to coat well. Bake, uncovered, at 450 degrees for 10 minutes or until shrimp turn pink. Serve immediately. Makes 6 servings.

Casual Entrées

Page 84

For easy weeknight meals or small get togethers with friends, try these simple but satisfying main dishes. Guests will leave with smiles on their faces, and you'll spend less time in the kitchen and plenty of time celebrating the season.

Fabulous Fajitas,
page 82

Family Swiss Steak

1½ lbs. round steak
3 T. all-purpose flour
1 T. fresh parsley, chopped
¼ t. dried thyme
⅛ t. pepper

2 T. vegetable oil
½ c. sliced onion
2 carrots, cut in strips
10¾-oz. can French onion soup

Pound steak to ¼-inch thickness with a meat mallet or rolling pin; cut into pieces. Stir together flour, parsley, thyme and pepper in a 9" pie plate. Coat steak with flour mixture.

Heat oil in a large skillet over medium heat. Add steak and brown 3 to 4 minutes on each side; add onion, carrots and soup. Reduce heat to low; cover and cook 50 more minutes or until steak is tender. Makes 4 servings.

Cranberry Meat Loaves

1 lb. ground beef
1 c. cooked rice
½ c. tomato juice
¼ c. minced onion
1 egg

1 t. salt
16-oz. can whole-berry cranberry sauce
⅓ c. brown sugar, packed
1 T. lemon juice

Mix together ground beef, rice, tomato juice, onion, egg and salt. Shape mixture evenly into 5 mini meat loaves and place in a greased 13"x9" pan.

Mix together cranberry sauce, brown sugar and lemon juice; spoon over top of each loaf. Bake at 350 degrees for 45 minutes. Makes 5 servings.

Stroganoff Skillet

1 lb. ground beef
1 onion, chopped
10¾-oz. can cream of mushroom soup

3 c. wide egg noodles, uncooked
1 c. sour cream
1 c. beef broth
½ c. water

Brown ground beef and onion in a large skillet over medium heat; drain and return meat mixture to skillet. Gradually add soup and remaining ingredients. Bring to a boil; cover, reduce heat and simmer for 10 minutes or until noodles are tender. Makes 4 to 6 servings.

Slow-Cooker Lasagna

1 lb. ground beef
1 t. dried Italian seasoning
28-oz. jar spaghetti sauce
⅓ c. water
8 lasagna noodles, uncooked

4½-oz. jar mushrooms
15-oz. container ricotta cheese
2 c. shredded part-skim
   mozzarella cheese, divided

This recipe is so easy, you may never go back to the conventional method with boiled noodles and complicated assembly. Avoid the temptation to sneak a peek at your recipe or taste it during cooking. It takes about 20 minutes for the heat to build back up to the previous temperature once the lid is removed.

Cook ground beef and Italian seasoning in a large skillet over medium-high heat, stirring until beef crumbles; drain. Combine spaghetti sauce and water in a small bowl.

Place 4 uncooked noodles in bottom of a lightly greased 5-quart electric slow cooker. Layer with half each of beef mixture, spaghetti sauce mixture and mushrooms.

Spread ricotta cheese over mushrooms. Sprinkle with one cup mozzarella cheese. Layer with remaining noodles, beef, spaghetti sauce mixture, mushrooms and mozzarella cheese. Cover and cook on high heat one hour; turn heat to low and cook 5 hours. Makes 4 servings.

Fast Facts for Slow Cooking

Time is on your side when you use a slow cooker. With 4 to 8 hours of free time while your supper cooks, the possibilities are endless. Here are some helpful hints.

•Always start meat or poultry dishes on high heat for the first hour of cooking to speed up the time it takes to reach a safe temperature. Then reduce to low heat for the duration of the cooking time.

•Cut whole chickens and cuts of meat over 2 pounds in half before cooking to make sure they cook thoroughly and evenly.

•To speed up a recipe that calls for cooking on low heat, remember that one hour on high heat equals 2 hours on low heat. Low heat is best for all-day cooking.

•Vegetables generally cook slower than most meats. Most vegetables should be thinly sliced or placed near the sides or bottom of the slow cooker.

Spaghetti Sauce & Meatballs

1 medium onion, chopped
3 T. olive oil
1 clove garlic, minced
14½-oz. can diced tomatoes with
   basil, garlic and oregano,
   undrained
2 (6-oz.) cans tomato paste
1½ c. water

1 to 3 t. sugar
1½ t. salt
1½ t. dried oregano
½ t. pepper
1 bay leaf
Meatballs
6 c. hot cooked pasta

Sauté onion in hot oil in a Dutch oven over medium-high heat 3 minutes or until tender. Add garlic; sauté one minute. Stir in tomatoes, tomato paste and next 6 ingredients. Reduce heat; simmer, uncovered, 30 minutes. Remove bay leaf; add Meatballs and cook 30 more minutes. Serve sauce and Meatballs over pasta. Makes 4 servings.

Meatballs

1 lb. ground chuck
1 c. freshly prepared bread crumbs
½ c. grated Romano cheese
2 T. fresh parsley, chopped
1 T. water
1 t. salt

1 t. dried oregano
¼ t. pepper
1 clove garlic, minced
2 eggs, lightly beaten
2 T. vegetable oil

Combine first 10 ingredients in a large bowl; mix well. Shape mixture into 20 (1½-inch) balls.

Cook meatballs in hot oil in a large skillet over medium-high heat 10 minutes or until browned. Makes 20 meatballs.

Pork Chops & Rice Skillet

4 (1-inch-thick) pork chops (about
   1⅓ lbs.)
1 t. salt, divided
½ t. pepper, divided
¼ t. garlic powder
2 T. vegetable oil
1¼ c. water

¾ c. long-grain rice, uncooked
¾ c. chopped onion
15¼-oz. can whole kernel corn,
   drained
14½-oz. can diced tomatoes,
   drained

Sprinkle pork chops evenly with ½ teaspoon salt, ¼ teaspoon pepper and ¼ teaspoon garlic powder. Heat oil in a large skillet over medium-high heat; add pork chops. Cook 2 to 3 minutes on each side or until browned. Remove pork chops and set aside.

Add water, rice, onion and remaining ½ teaspoon salt to skillet; stir to combine. Place pork chops on top of rice mixture. Top rice and pork chops evenly with corn and tomatoes. Sprinkle with remaining ¼ teaspoon pepper. Bring to a boil; reduce heat, cover, and simmer 20 to 25 minutes or until rice is tender and pork chops are done. Let stand 5 minutes before serving. Makes 4 servings.

Chunky Ham Pot Pie

1 lb. new potatoes, coarsely chopped
10-oz. pkg. frozen cut broccoli or
   flowerets
2 T. butter or margarine
1 c. chopped onion
10¾-oz. can cream of potato soup,
   undiluted
8-oz. container sour cream
1 c. shredded sharp Cheddar cheese

¾ c. milk
½ t. garlic powder
½ t. salt
¼ t. pepper
2½ c. chopped honey-baked ham or
   other ham
½ (15-oz.) pkg. refrigerated pie
   crusts

Feed your family this pot pie brimming with ham, veggies and Cheddar cheese. You can divide this pot pie into two 2-quart dishes. Bake one now, and freeze one for later. You will need the whole package of pie crusts for two casseroles. Top the casserole to be frozen with crust before freezing, but do not cut slits in top until ready to bake. Let frozen casserole stand at room temperature 20 minutes before baking.

Cook chopped potatoes in boiling water to cover 10 minutes or until barely tender; drain. Meanwhile, cook broccoli according to package directions; drain.

Melt butter in a large skillet over medium heat; add onion. Cook 10 minutes or until onion is tender and begins to brown, stirring often.

Combine soup and next 6 ingredients in a large bowl, stirring well. Stir in onion, potatoes, broccoli and ham. Spoon ham mixture into a greased 3½-quart baking dish. (If desired, cover and chill overnight. Let stand at room temperature 30 minutes before baking.)

Unfold pie crust onto a lightly floured surface and press out fold lines. Roll pastry to extend ¾ inches beyond edges of casserole. Place pastry over ham mixture. Seal edges and crimp. Cut slits in top of pastry to allow steam to escape. Bake, uncovered, at 400 degrees for 45 minutes or until crust is golden. Let stand 10 minutes before serving. Makes 6 to 8 servings.

Red Beans & Rice

(pictured on opposite page)

This recipe takes a shortcut by using canned beans in place of dried…we loved the flavor and simplicity of this version of the traditional New Orleans dish. Kick it up a notch by using andouille sausage and shaking a few drops of hot sauce on top!

1 lb. Kielbasa, cut into ¼-inch slices
1 medium onion, chopped
1 green pepper, chopped
1 clove garlic, minced
2 (16-oz.) cans dark kidney beans, drained

14.5-oz. can diced tomatoes
½ t. dried oregano
½ t. black pepper
4 c. hot cooked rice

Cook sausage in a Dutch oven over low heat 6 minutes, stirring often. Add onion, green pepper and garlic; cook over medium-high heat 5 minutes or until tender. Add beans, tomatoes, oregano and black pepper; reduce heat and simmer, uncovered, 20 minutes, stirring occasionally. Serve over rice. Makes 4 to 6 servings.

Sausage & Wild Rice Casserole

This meaty casserole topped with toasted nuts makes a hearty contribution to breakfast or dinner.

6-oz. pkg. long-grain and wild rice mix
1 lb. hot ground pork sausage
1 lb. ground beef
1 large onion, chopped
8-oz. pkg. sliced mushrooms

8-oz. can sliced water chestnuts, drained
⅓ c. fresh parsley, chopped
3 T. soy sauce
2.25-oz. pkg. sliced natural almonds

Cook rice mix according to package directions.

Meanwhile, cook sausage and ground beef in a large skillet, stirring until it crumbles and is no longer pink. Drain and pat dry with paper towels. Cook onion and mushrooms in same skillet over medium heat 7 minutes or until tender, stirring occasionally.

Combine rice, sausage and beef, onion and mushrooms, water chestnuts, parsley and soy sauce; stir well. Spoon sausage mixture into an ungreased 13"x9" baking dish. Sprinkle with almonds. Bake, uncovered, at 350 degrees for 20 minutes or until thoroughly heated. Makes 8 to 10 servings.

Note: *To make ahead, spoon sausage mixture into baking dish and cover and chill overnight. The next day, remove from refrigerator and let stand at room temperature 30 minutes. Then bake, uncovered, at 350 degrees for 30 minutes or until thoroughly heated.*

Fabulous Fajitas

(pictured on page 75)

⭐⭐⭐

Make-ahead simplicity and delicious taste make these fajitas a family favorite. To warm tortillas, wrap them in aluminum foil and bake at 325 degrees for 15 minutes or until thoroughly heated.

1 lb. boneless, skinless chicken breasts, cut into strips
2 T. cornstarch
2 T. lemon juice
1 t. garlic powder
1 t. seasoned salt
½ t. dried oregano
½ t. black pepper
⅛ t. liquid barbecue smoke seasoning

2 T. vegetable oil
1 green pepper, cut into strips
1 onion, halved and thinly sliced
1 tomato, cut into thin wedges
½ c. salsa
8 (8-inch) flour tortillas, warmed
Salsa
Sour Cream

Combine first 8 ingredients in a medium bowl or heavy-duty plastic zipping bag. Cover or seal; marinate at least 2 hours or up 24 hours. Remove chicken and discard marinade.

Sauté chicken in oil in a large skillet 6 minutes or until done. Add green pepper and onion; cook 4 minutes or until crisp-tender. Add tomato and ½ cup salsa; simmer one to 2 minutes or until thoroughly heated. Divide mixture evenly among tortillas. Roll up tortillas; top each serving with additional salsa and sour cream. Serve immediately. Makes 8 servings.

Herbed Chicken Pizzas

This pizza also makes an easy, filling snack when the occasion calls for substantial hors d'oeuvres. Cut each pizza into 6 wedges for a yield of 24 appetizer servings.

2 (3-oz.) pkgs. cream cheese, softened
¼ c. fines herbes soup mix
2 T. white vinegar or white balsamic vinegar
1 clove garlic, crushed

2 (8-oz.) pkgs. Italian pizza crusts
½ c. sun-dried tomatoes packed in oil, drained and thinly sliced
1 deli-roasted chicken breast, finely shredded (about 2 c.)
1½ c. shredded mozzarella cheese

Process first 4 ingredients in a food processor until smooth, stopping once to scrape down sides (or beat first 4 ingredients at medium speed with an electric mixer until smooth).

Spread mixture evenly over pizza crusts. Sprinkle with tomatoes, chicken and mozzarella. Place pizzas on a baking sheet. Bake at 400 degrees for 10 minutes or until cheese melts. Makes 4 pizzas.

Chicken Scampi

4 to 6 cloves garlic, pressed
2 T. fresh oregano, chopped
2 T. fresh parsley, chopped
2 T. lemon juice
1 t. garlic powder
½ t. salt
½ c. olive oil

¼ c. dry white wine or chicken
  broth
¼ c. chili sauce
2 boneless, skinless chicken
  breasts, cut into bite-size pieces
Cooked angel hair pasta
Grated Romano cheese

Combine first 10 ingredients in a large mixing bowl. Place in a greased 8"x8" baking dish. Bake, uncovered, at 450 degrees for 12 to 14 minutes or until chicken is done. Serve over angel hair pasta and sprinkle with grated Romano cheese. Makes 2 servings.

Flavorful garlic, white wine and fresh herbs contribute the traditional flavors of shrimp scampi to this scrumptious chicken dish. Try adding fresh broccoli and sliced mushrooms for variety.

Creamy Chicken à la King

★ ★ ★

This hearty dish can also be served over rice, mashed potatoes or hot biscuits.

1 c. fresh mushrooms, sliced
5 T. butter or margarine, divided
½ red pepper, seeded and diced
¾ c. fresh or frozen peas
¼ c. all-purpose flour
32-oz. carton chicken broth

3 c. cooked cubed chicken
½ c. sliced cooked carrots
1 T. fresh parsley, minced
Salt and black pepper to taste
8 oz. wide egg noodles, cooked

Sauté mushrooms in one tablespoon butter until tender; set aside.

Cook red pepper and peas in a small saucepan of boiling water to cover for 2 minutes; rinse in cold water.

Melt remaining 4 tablespoons of butter in a large saucepan; add flour, whisking 2 minutes or until smooth. Slowly add chicken broth, whisking thoroughly; simmer about 5 minutes or until thickened. Add chicken, carrots, mushrooms, red pepper, peas, parsley and seasonings. Simmer 5 more minutes, thinning with additional chicken broth or water, if necessary. Serve over hot buttered noodles. Makes 4 servings.

Leslie's Favorite Chicken & Wild Rice Casserole

To make and freeze this casserole ahead, freeze it unbaked up to one month. Remove from freezer and let stand at room temperature one hour. Bake, covered, at 350 degrees for 30 minutes. Uncover and bake 55 more minutes. Sprinkle with cheese and bake 5 more minutes.

2 (6.2-oz.) pkgs. fast-cooking long-grain and wild rice mix
¼ c. butter or margarine
4 celery ribs, chopped
2 medium onions, chopped
2 (8-oz.) cans sliced water chestnuts, drained
5 c. chopped cooked chicken
4 c. shredded Cheddar cheese, divided

2 (10¾-oz.) cans cream of mushroom soup, undiluted
2 (8-oz.) containers sour cream
1 c. milk
½ t. salt
½ t. pepper
½ c. freshly prepared bread crumbs
2.25-oz. pkg. sliced almonds, toasted

Prepare rice mixes according to package directions.

Melt butter in a large skillet over medium heat; add celery and onions. Sauté 10 minutes or until tender. Stir in water chestnuts, rice, chicken, 3 cups cheese and next 5 ingredients.

Spoon mixture into a lightly greased 15"x 10" baking dish or a 4-quart casserole. Top casserole with bread crumbs. Bake, uncovered, at 350 degrees for 35 minutes. Sprinkle with remaining one cup cheese and almonds; bake 5 more minutes. Makes 10 to 12 servings.

Green Chilie-Turkey Pot Pie

⭐ ⭐ ⭐

2 bunches green onions, chopped
  (about 1½ c.)
3 T. vegetable oil
2 (4.5-oz.) cans chopped green
  chilies, undrained
2.25-oz. can sliced ripe olives,
  drained
¼ c. all-purpose flour
1½ t. cumin
2 (16-oz.) cans pinto beans,
  rinsed and drained

14-oz. can chicken broth
2 c. chopped cooked turkey breast
1 c. all-purpose flour
1½ t. baking powder
2 c. shredded Mexican four-cheese
  blend
⅔ c. milk
1 egg, lightly beaten

This one-dish pot pie is the ultimate in easy. You just spoon the cheesy biscuit topping over the turkey, bean and green chilie filling, and bake.

Sauté green onions in oil in a Dutch oven over medium heat one minute. Add green chilies and next 3 ingredients; cook 2 minutes, stirring constantly. Stir in beans and broth; bring to a boil. Reduce heat and simmer, stirring constantly, 5 to 7 minutes or until mixture is thickened. Stir in turkey. Pour into a greased 13"x9" baking dish.

Combine one cup flour and baking powder in a small bowl. Add cheese, milk and egg, stirring just until blended. Spread biscuit topping over filling, leaving a one-inch border around edge.

Bake, uncovered, at 375 degrees for 30 minutes or until topping is golden and pot pie is bubbly. Makes 6 servings.

Shiitake Mushroom & Spinach Manicotti

This creamy, crusty-topped casserole is a great make-ahead option for the holiday rush. Cover and chill at least 8 hours before baking. Remove from refrigerator and let stand at room temperature 30 minutes. Bake as directed.

12 manicotti or cannelloni shells
¼ c. butter or margarine, divided
4½ c. sliced shiitake or other mushrooms
2 cloves garlic, minced
10-oz. pkg. fresh spinach, coarse stems removed
1 c. ricotta cheese
3 oz. freshly grated Parmesan cheese
1 egg, beaten

½ t. salt
½ t. pepper
⅓ c. butter or margarine
2 T. all-purpose flour
2 c. half-and-half
½ t. salt
1 c. shredded Gouda cheese
2 slices 7-grain sandwich bread
1½ c. shredded Mexican four-cheese blend
3 T. butter or margarine, melted

Cook shells according to package directions; drain.

Meanwhile, melt 3 tablespoons butter in a large skillet; add mushrooms and garlic and sauté until mushroom liquid is absorbed. Transfer mushroom mixture to a large bowl.

Melt remaining one tablespoon butter in skillet. Add spinach; cover and cook over medium-low heat 5 minutes or until spinach wilts. Add spinach to mushroom mixture. Stir in ricotta cheese and next 4 ingredients. Spoon spinach mixture evenly into cooked shells. Place stuffed shells in a greased 13"x9" baking dish.

Melt ⅓ cup butter in a heavy saucepan over low heat; whisk in flour until smooth. Cook one minute, whisking constantly. Gradually whisk in half-and-half; cook over medium heat, whisking constantly, until mixture is thickened and bubbly. Stir in ½ teaspoon salt. Add Gouda cheese, stirring until cheese melts. Pour over stuffed shells.

Process bread in a blender or food processor until it resembles coarse crumbs. Spread crumbs in a small pan; bake at 350 degrees for 3 to 4 minutes or until toasted.

Combine toasted crumbs, cheese blend and 3 tablespoons melted butter in a bowl; toss well and sprinkle over shells. Bake, uncovered, at 350 degrees for 45 minutes or until bubbly. Makes 6 servings.

Spicy Pasta Alfredo Casserole

★ ★ ★

12-oz. pkg. fettuccine, uncooked
2 (1.6-oz.) pkg. Alfredo sauce mix
2 c. milk
1 c. water
2 T. butter or margarine
16-oz. container sour cream
10-oz. can diced tomatoes and green chilies, drained
14-oz. can quartered artichoke hearts, drained
12-oz. jar roasted red pepper, drained and chopped
1 c. freshly grated or finely shredded refrigerated Parmesan cheese

Sassy ingredients—tomatoes and green chilies, artichoke hearts, and roasted peppers—team up for a meatless main dish or a rich side to chicken, ham or beef.

Cook pasta according to package directions; drain well. Set aside.

Combine sauce mix and next 3 ingredients in a large saucepan; bring to a boil over medium heat, stirring constantly. Reduce heat; cook, stirring constantly, 2 minutes or until sauce is thickened and bubbly. Stir in sour cream and tomatoes and green chilies.

Combine pasta, sauce mixture, artichokes and red pepper; spoon mixture into a greased 13"x9" baking dish. (If desired, cover and chill overnight. Let stand at room temperature 30 minutes before baking.)

Cover and bake at 350 degrees for one hour. Uncover casserole and sprinkle with cheese; bake, uncovered, 10 more minutes or until cheese is lightly browned. Makes 6 main-dish servings or 10 side-dish servings.

Christmas Morning Delights

Page 94

Your whole family will be
bright eyed and bushy tailed when
they wake up to the aromas of
these Christmas morning specialties.
But don't wait until the holidays to
try these morning delights...
they're good any time
of the year!

Ooey-Gooey Pancake
S'mores, page 94

Cream Cheese Scrambled Eggs

The addition of cream cheese helps produce creamy results.

12 eggs
1 c. half-and-half or milk
2 (3-oz.) pkgs. cream cheese, cubed
¾ t. salt
¼ t. pepper
¼ c. butter or margarine
Chopped fresh chives

Process first 5 ingredients in a blender until frothy, stopping to scrape down sides.

Melt butter in a large heavy skillet over medium heat; reduce heat to medium-low. Add egg mixture and cook, without stirring, until mixture begins to set on bottom. Draw a spatula across bottom of skillet to form large curds. Continue cooking until eggs are thickened but still moist; don't stir constantly. Sprinkle with chives. Makes 6 to 8 servings.

Christmas Breakfast Stratas

These casseroles can be partially made ahead and assembled just before cooking. Cook the sausage a day ahead and store in a plastic zipping bag in the refrigerator. The bread can also be cubed a day ahead and stored at room temperature in a plastic zipping bag. These casseroles can also be made in two 11"x7" baking dishes.

2 (1-lb.) pkgs. hot pork sausage
16-oz. loaf sliced French bread, cut into 1-inch cubes
4 c. shredded Cheddar and Monterey Jack cheese blend, divided
8-oz. pkg. sliced mushrooms, coarsely chopped
4½-oz. can diced green chilies, drained
4-oz. can sliced ripe olives, drained
8 eggs, lightly beaten
4 c. milk
1 t. salt
1 t. onion powder
1 t. dry mustard
1 t. dried oregano
¼ t. pepper
Garnishes: sour cream, salsa

Cook sausage in a large skillet over medium-high heat, stirring until it crumbles and is no longer pink. Drain and set aside.

Divide bread cubes among a lightly greased 13"x9" baking dish and an 8"x8" baking dish. Divide 2 cups cheese over bread cubes. Sprinkle with cooked sausage, mushrooms, green chilies and olives.

Whisk together eggs and next 6 ingredients in a medium bowl. Pour mixture over casseroles. Sprinkle with remaining 2 cups cheese. Bake, uncovered, at 350 degrees for one hour or until set. Garnish with sour cream and salsa, if desired. Makes 20 servings.

Casual Christmas Breakfast
Here's an idea to start off the Christmas day fun! Get the family involved in making biscuits from scratch and stirring the scrambled eggs as they cook. Start a bowl of ambrosia the night before and do the prep work for Christmas Breakfast Stratas. While the biscuits bake, let the coffee perk and the children peek in their stockings.

Mediterranean Frittata

8 pitted kalamata olives, chopped
1 medium zucchini, cut into
  ½-inch cubes
1 red pepper, diced
½ c. chopped onion
¼ c. olive oil
9 eggs, lightly beaten
½ (4-oz.) pkg. feta cheese,
  crumbled

⅓ c. thinly sliced fresh basil
½ t. salt
½ t. pepper
⅓ c. freshly grated Parmesan
  cheese
Garnish: fresh basil sprigs

★ ★ ★

Serve this versatile egg dish with a light salad for supper or with fruit for brunch.

Cook first 4 ingredients in hot oil in a 10" oven-proof skillet over medium-high heat, stirring constantly, until vegetables are tender.

Combine eggs and next 4 ingredients; pour into skillet over vegetables. Cover and cook over medium-low heat 10 to 12 minutes or until almost set. Remove from heat and sprinkle with Parmesan cheese.

Broil 5½ inches from heat 2 to 3 minutes or until golden. Cut frittata into wedges; garnish, if desired. Serve warm or at room temperature. Makes 6 servings.

Brunch Egg Squares

Make this baked egg casserole a new tradition for your Christmas morning breakfast. With under 10 minutes of work, this casserole will have you in and out of the kitchen quickly to enjoy all the festivities.

3 c. shredded Cheddar cheese
3 c. shredded mozzarella cheese
2 T. butter or margarine
¾ c. sliced fresh mushrooms
½ c. sliced green onions

8 oz. diced cooked ham
½ c. all-purpose flour
1¾ c. milk
8 eggs
2 T. fresh parsley, chopped

Combine cheeses in a medium bowl; sprinkle ½ of cheese in an ungreased 13"x9" baking dish.

Melt butter in a large skillet over medium-high heat. Add mushrooms and onions; sauté 4 minutes or until liquid evaporates. Spoon vegetable mixture over cheese in baking dish; top with ham and remaining cheese.

Whisk together flour and remaining 3 ingredients in a large bowl; pour over cheese.

Bake, uncovered, at 350 degrees for 45 to 50 minutes or until set. Let stand 10 minutes before serving. Makes 8 to 10 servings.

Christmas Morn' Casserole

20-oz. pkg. frozen hash browns,
  thawed
4 c. shredded Monterey Jack cheese
2 c. diced cooked ham

7 eggs
1 c. milk
½ t. salt
½ t. ground mustard

Place hash browns in a greased 13"x9" baking dish. Sprinkle with cheese and ham; set aside. Beat together eggs, milk, salt and mustard; pour over ham. Bake, covered, at 350 degrees for one hour. Uncover and bake 15 more minutes or until golden. Makes 8 servings.

This casserole is ready to bake in only 15 minutes, so you can get back to all the Christmas morning fun!

Three-Cheese Spinach Quiche

½ (17¼-oz.) pkg. frozen puff pastry
  sheets, thawed
10-oz. pkg. frozen chopped
  spinach
1 c. whipping cream
½ t. pepper
¼ t. salt

3 eggs, lightly beaten
1½ c. shredded mozzarella cheese
½ c. shredded Cheddar cheese
½ c. finely chopped onion
7-oz. jar roasted red peppers,
  drained and chopped
½ c. crumbled feta cheese

Christmas colors of red and green rise to the top of this creamy quiche that has a flaky crust . . . it's perfect to serve during the holidays!

Unfold pastry sheet onto a lightly floured surface. Roll into a 13-inch square. Place in a lightly greased 9" deep-dish pie plate. Fold edges under and crimp. Prick pastry lightly with a fork. Freeze at least 15 minutes to make pastry firmer. Bake pastry at 400 degrees for 12 minutes. Let cool on a wire rack.

Reduce oven temperature to 350 degrees. Cook spinach according to package directions. Squeeze spinach between several layers of paper towels to remove excess moisture. Combine spinach, cream, ½ teaspoon pepper, salt and eggs, stirring well.

Sprinkle mozzarella and Cheddar cheeses and onion into pastry shell. Add spinach mixture. Top with red pepper; sprinkle with feta cheese. Bake, uncovered, at 350 degrees for 55 minutes or until set. Cover loosely with aluminum foil and let stand 30 minutes before serving. Makes 6 to 8 servings.

Invite your neighbors over for a holiday breakfast. Welcome them with steaming mugs of cider, Christmas music and a crackling fire. Serve hearty favorites buffet-style and chat about your holiday plans. It's a fun way to enjoy each other's company!

Blueberry & Cheese Streusel

2⅓ c. all-purpose flour
1⅓ c. sugar
2 t. baking powder
1 t. salt
¾ c. butter or margarine, cut into
    pieces
¾ c. milk
2 eggs, lightly beaten
1 t. vanilla extract

1 c. fresh blueberries
1 c. ricotta cheese
1 egg, lightly beaten
2 T. sugar
1 T. grated lemon rind
½ c. chopped pecans
⅓ c. brown sugar, packed
1 t. cinnamon

Combine first 5 ingredients with a pastry blender or 2 knives until crumbly. Set aside one cup crumb mixture.

Add milk, 2 eggs and vanilla to remaining crumb mixture. Beat at medium speed with an electric mixer 2 minutes. Pour batter into a lightly greased 13"x9" pan; layer blueberries over batter. Combine ricotta cheese, one egg, 2 tablespoons sugar and lemon rind. Spoon over blueberries, spreading mixture to cover blueberries. Stir together reserved crumb mixture, pecans, brown sugar and cinnamon; sprinkle over cheese mixture.

Bake at 350 degrees for 50 to 52 minutes or until a toothpick inserted in center comes out clean. Makes 16 servings.

Ooey-Gooey Pancake S'mores

(pictured on page 89)

Bring the outdoors in with a plate of these chocolatey pancakes. Kids of all ages will have fun assembling these ooey-gooey breakfast treats. All that's missing from these s'mores is the campfire!

2 c. biscuit baking mix
1⅓ c. milk
2 T. sugar
1 t. vanilla extract
1 egg
12 T. coarsely crushed graham
    cracker crumbs, divided

12 T. marshmallow creme, divided
12 T. semi-sweet chocolate chips,
    divided
Garnish: graham crackers crumbs,
    semi-sweet chocolate chips

Combine first 5 ingredients in a medium bowl, stirring just until dry ingredients are moistened.

For each pancake, pour ¼ cup batter onto a hot, lightly greased griddle. Sprinkle one tablespoon graham cracker crumbs over each pancake. Cook pancakes until edges are covered with small bubbles; turn and cook other side.

For each serving, spread one tablespoon marshmallow creme over crumb side of one pancake. Sprinkle one tablespoon chocolate chips over marshmallow creme. Top with another pancake and repeat toppings. Top with another pancake and one tablespoon marshmallow creme. Garnish each stack, if desired. Serve immediately. Makes 4 servings (12 [5-inch] pancakes).

Peaches & Cream French Toast

8-oz. loaf French bread, sliced into
  8 (2-inch) slices
3-oz. pkg. cream cheese, softened
3 T. peach preserves
1 T. brown sugar
3 eggs

½ c. milk
½ t. vanilla extract
¼ t. cinnamon
Maple syrup
2 T. powdered sugar

Cut a horizontal pocket into top crust of each bread slice; do not cut through.

Beat cream cheese, preserves and brown sugar in a small bowl at medium speed with an electric mixer until creamy. Spoon about one tablespoon cream cheese mixture into each bread pocket.

Whisk together eggs, milk, vanilla and cinnamon; dip stuffed bread slices into mixture, coating all sides.

Heat a large skillet coated with non-stick vegetable spray over medium-high heat until hot. Cook bread slices, in batches, 2 minutes on each side or until golden. Serve with maple syrup and sprinkle with powdered sugar. Makes 4 servings.

Cream cheese, peach preserves and brown sugar nestle between two generous slices of French bread, making an unforgettable breakfast. Top with warm maple syrup and a dusting of powdered sugar. If you want to get ahead of the game, stuff the bread slices the night before you're making the French toast and chill them.

Orange Biscuits

"My grandmother kept a journal and always included lots of recipes alongside her memories. I remember her always serving these biscuits with ham and oh, the aroma from the kitchen was wonderful."
–Peg Baker
La Rue, OH

¾ c. sugar, divided
½ c. orange juice
¼ c. butter or margarine
2 t. orange zest
2 c. all-purpose flour
1 T. baking powder
½ t. salt
¼ c. shortening
¾ c. milk
¼ c. butter or margarine, melted
½ t. cinnamon

Combine ½ cup sugar, orange juice, 1/4 cup butter and orange zest in a medium saucepan. Cook and stir over medium heat 2 to 3 minutes. Pour orange mixture evenly into 12 lightly greased muffin cups; set aside.

Combine flour, baking powder and salt; cut in shortening with a pastry blender or 2 knives until mixture resembles coarse crumbs. Add milk to flour mixture, stirring just until moist.

Turn dough out onto a lightly floured surface and knead 3 or 4 times. Roll dough into a 9-inch square (about ¼- to ⅓-inch thickness); brush with ¼ cup melted butter.

Combine remaining ¼ cup sugar and cinnamon; sprinkle over dough. Roll up jelly roll fashion, pinching edges to seal. Cut into 12 slices. Place slices, cut side down, over orange sauce in muffin cups. Bake at 450 degrees for 13 to 14 minutes or until lightly browned. Makes one dozen.

Streusel Cran-Orange Muffins

(pictured opposite on bottom plate)

1½ c. all-purpose flour
1 t. baking powder
½ t. baking soda
½ t. salt
1 egg, lightly beaten
½ c. cranberry-orange relish
1 t. grated orange zest
⅓ c. freshly squeezed orange juice
¼ c. brown sugar, packed
¼ c. butter or margarine, melted
⅓ c. chopped pecans
¼ c. brown sugar, packed
½ t. cinnamon

Combine first 4 ingredients in a large bowl; make a well in center of mixture. Combine egg and next 5 ingredients; add to dry ingredients, stirring just until moistened. Spoon into greased muffin pans, filling 2/3 full.

Combine pecans, ¼ cup brown sugar and cinnamon; sprinkle over muffins. Bake at 400 degrees for 15 minutes or until golden. Remove from pans immediately. Makes one dozen.

Savory Sausage-Swiss Muffins

(pictured above on top plate)

½ lb. mild or spicy ground pork
  sausage
1¾ c. biscuit baking mix
½ c. shredded Swiss cheese

¾ t. ground sage
¼ t. dried thyme
1 egg, lightly beaten
½ c. milk

Brown sausage in a skillet over medium heat, stirring until it crumbles. Drain well.

Combine sausage, biscuit mix and next 3 ingredients in a bowl; make a well in center of mixture.

Combine egg and milk; add to dry ingredients, stirring just until dry ingredients are moistened. Spoon batter into greased muffin pans, filling pans ⅔ full. Bake at 375 degrees for 22 minutes or until golden. Serve warm. Makes one dozen.

Store any leftover muffins in the refrigerator. Then, reheat leftovers in the microwave; one muffin heats in 20 to 30 seconds at high power (100%).

Holiday Sideboard

Page 108

Round out your holiday meal with this smorgasbord of salads and side dishes. You'll find familiar favorites along with sensational new sides sure to become part of your holiday traditions.

Christmas Eve Salad,
page 100

Apple-Cranberry Salad

⅔ c. sour cream
⅓ c. mayonnaise
2 c. peeled, cored and cubed apples
2 t. lemon juice

½ c. dried cranberries
½ c. seedless green grapes, halved
½ c. chopped walnuts
½ c. chopped celery

Combine sour cream and mayonnaise in a small bowl; set aside. Gently toss apples in lemon juice in a large bowl. Stir in cranberries and remaining 3 ingredients. Add sour cream dressing; toss to coat. Cover and chill at least one hour before serving. Makes 8 servings.

Christmas Eve Salad

(pictured on page 99)

A bounty of apples, kiwi, oranges and strawberries make up this colorful salad. Crown it in seasonal style with star-shaped croutons. Try different cookie cutter shapes to make festive croutons for anytime of the year.

¼ c. chopped almonds
1 T. plus 1 t. sugar
1 Gala apple, thinly sliced
1 kiwi fruit, sliced
11-oz. can mandarin oranges, drained
1 c. sliced strawberries
3 c. torn iceberg lettuce
1 small head romaine lettuce, torn

2 stalks celery, thinly sliced
5 green onions, sliced
¼ c. vegetable oil
2 T. white vinegar
1 T. fresh parsley, chopped
2 T. sugar
½ t. salt
⅛ t. pepper
Star Croutons

Cook almonds and sugar in a skillet over medium heat, stirring constantly, until almonds are golden. Pour onto wax paper; cool. Break almonds into pieces.
Combine fruit, lettuces, celery and onions in a large bowl.
Whisk together oil, vinegar, parsley, sugar, salt and pepper in a small bowl. Pour dressing mixture over salad; toss gently. Sprinkle with almonds and Star Croutons; serve immediately. Makes 8 servings.

Star Croutons

6 slices firm white bread
2 T. butter or margarine

1 T. olive oil
1 clove garlic, pressed

Use a 1½-inch star cookie cutter to cut out stars from bread. (You should get about 6 stars from each slice of bread.) Place stars in a medium bowl.
Combine butter, olive oil and garlic in a small bowl. Microwave on high power (100%) about 30 seconds or until butter melts. Stir until well blended.
Drizzle melted butter mixture over bread stars; toss until well coated. Arrange stars in a single layer on an ungreased baking sheet. Bake at 350 degrees for 12 minutes or until golden. Makes 3 dozen.

Making Magic

•Gilded fruit and vegetables add sparkle and elegance to your holiday centerpieces. With gold spray paint, give a festive touch to artichokes, mini pumpkins, gourds and pomegranates. Make sure you spray paint in a well-ventilated area or outdoors.

•Make sugared fruit (for decoration only) by brushing apples, grapes, pears and plums with beaten egg white and then sprinkling them with sugar. Let coated fruit dry on wire racks. Sugared fruit looks pretty and frosty when placed in a bowl with some greenery tucked in. Place the bowl on a lace doily.

Cashew Salad

1 head lettuce, torn
8-oz. pkg. shredded Swiss cheese
1 c. vegetable oil
¾ c. sugar
⅓ c. white vinegar
Salt to taste

1 t. mustard
1 t. grated onion
1 T. poppy seeds
1 c. cashews
1 c. croutons
Garnish: additional croutons

Toss together lettuce and Swiss cheese in a medium serving bowl. Whisk together oil, sugar, vinegar, salt, mustard, onion and poppy seeds. To serve, toss together cashews, croutons, dressing and lettuce mixture. Garnish with additional croutons, if desired. Makes 6 to 8 servings.

"A wonderfully crunchy salad!"

*–Kate Saunier
Grand Rapids, MI*

Winter Salad

1 bunch broccoli, cut into small
  pieces
1 head cauliflower, cut into small
  pieces
1 medium red onion, thinly sliced
  and separated in rings
8-oz. pkg. sliced mushrooms

¼ c. raisins (optional)
½ lb. bacon, crisply cooked and
  crumbled
1½ c. mayonnaise
⅓ c. sugar
3 T. white vinegar
Toasted almonds

Toss together first 6 ingredients. Whisk together mayonnaise, sugar and vinegar. Add dressing to vegetable mixture and refrigerate at least one to 2 hours before serving. Sprinkle with toasted almonds. Makes 8 to 10 servings.

"A hearty salad, full of vitamins!"

*–Barbara Bargdill
Delaware, OH*

Tempting Caesar Salad

1 clove garlic, cut in half
4 anchovy filets
¾ c. extra virgin olive oil
6 T. fresh lemon juice
1 t. pepper
½ t. salt
¼ c. red wine vinegar

½ c. egg substitute
1 large head romaine lettuce,
 torn into pieces
1 c. freshly grated Parmesan
 cheese
Croutons

Rub a wooden salad bowl with cut sides of garlic. Place anchovies in bowl; mash with a fork. Add olive oil and next 4 ingredients; stir well. Whisk egg substitute into mixture. Add lettuce; toss well. Sprinkle with cheese and Croutons. Makes 4 servings.

Croutons

3 T. olive oil
1 clove garlic, crushed

1 c. day-old French bread, cut into
 cubes

Heat oil and garlic in a large skillet over medium heat. Add bread cubes and sauté 3 to 4 minutes or until browned on all sides. Makes about 16 croutons.

Roasted Sweet Potato Salad

(pictured on opposite page)

Serve this salad chilled or at room temperature. Tossed in rosemary-honey vinaigrette, these golden potatoes come alive with flavor.

4 large sweet potatoes, peeled
 and cubed
2 T. olive oil, divided
¼ c. honey
3 T. white wine vinegar

2 T. chopped fresh rosemary
½ t. salt
½ t. pepper
2 cloves garlic, minced
Garnish: fresh rosemary sprig

Coat a large roasting pan with non-stick vegetable spray; toss together potatoes and one tablespoon oil in pan.

Bake, uncovered, at 450 degrees for 45 to 55 minutes or until potatoes are tender and roasted, stirring after 20 minutes.

Whisk together remaining one tablespoon oil, honey and next 5 ingredients. Transfer warm potatoes to a large serving bowl; add dressing and toss gently. Cool. Garnish, if desired. Makes 6 to 8 servings.

Hot Spiced Fruit

15¼-oz. can peach halves in heavy syrup
15-oz. can pear halves in heavy syrup
20-oz. can pineapple chunks in juice
½ c. orange marmalade
2 (3-inch) cinnamon sticks
1 t. nutmeg
1 t. ground cloves
2 T. cold butter or margarine, cut into pieces

"Serve this aromatic fruit side with your Christmas ham."
–Charlotte Wolfe
Ft. Lauderdale, FL

Drain fruit, reserving one cup juice. Spoon fruit into a 13"x9" baking dish. Combine reserved juice, marmalade and next 3 ingredients in a small saucepan over medium heat. Bring to a boil; boil one minute or until marmalade is melted, stirring constantly. Pour juice mixture over fruit; top with butter pieces.

Bake, uncovered, at 350 degrees for 30 minutes or until bubbly. Makes 8 to 10 servings.

Broccoli with 3-Cheese Horseradish Sauce

★ ★ ★

Horseradish and a little red pepper spike this cheesy sauce.

2 lbs. fresh broccoli
1 T. all-purpose flour
1½ c. whipping cream, divided
1 c. shredded sharp Cheddar
　cheese
1 c. shredded Monterey Jack
　cheese

2 T. grated Asiago or Parmesan
　cheese
1½ T. prepared horseradish
½ t. salt
¼ to ½ t. ground red pepper

Remove broccoli leaves and cut off tough ends of stalks; discard. Wash broccoli and cut into spears. Arrange spears in a steamer basket over boiling water. Cover and steam 8 to 10 minutes or until broccoli is crisp-tender.

Combine flour and ½ cup whipping cream in a saucepan, stirring until smooth. Stir in remaining one cup whipping cream. Cook over medium heat, stirring constantly, until thickened and bubbly. Add Cheddar cheese and remaining 5 ingredients; cook, stirring constantly, until cheeses melt. Spoon sauce over broccoli; serve hot. Makes 8 servings.

Brussels Sprouts au Gratin

¼ c. purchased plain bread crumbs
1 T. grated Parmesan cheese
2 lbs. fresh Brussels sprouts
2 T. butter or margarine
2 T. all-purpose flour
1½ c. milk
1 c. shredded Gruyère or Swiss
   cheese

1 T. white wine Worcestershire
   sauce
½ t. salt
¼ t. pepper
¼ t. paprika

Combine bread crumbs and Parmesan cheese; set aside.

Wash Brussels sprouts; remove discolored leaves. Trim ends and cut in half lengthwise. Cook Brussels sprouts in boiling water to cover 12 minutes or until barely tender. Drain and place in a lightly greased 1½-quart gratin dish or an 11"x7" baking dish. Set aside.

Melt butter in a saucepan over low heat; add flour, stirring until smooth. Cook, stirring constantly, one minute. Gradually add milk; cook over medium heat, stirring constantly, until thickened and bubbly.

Add Gruyère cheese and next 3 ingredients, stirring until cheese melts.

Spoon sauce over Brussels sprouts; sprinkle with bread crumb mixture and paprika. Bake, uncovered, at 350 degrees for 20 minutes or until browned and bubbly. Makes 8 servings.

Note: Three 10-ounce packages of frozen Brussels sprouts can be substituted for fresh sprouts, if desired. Just prepare according to package directions before assembling the casserole.

Homestyle Green Beans

(pictured on page 51)

2 lbs. fresh green beans, trimmed
   and cut into 1½-inch pieces
2 c. water
1 t. salt
⅓ c. butter or margarine
1½ T. sugar

1 t. dried basil
½ t. garlic powder
¼ t. salt
¼ t. pepper
2 c. halved cherry or grape
   tomatoes

Place beans in a Dutch oven; add water and salt. Bring to a boil; cover, reduce heat and simmer 15 minutes or until tender. Drain and keep warm.

Melt butter in a saucepan over medium heat; stir in sugar and next 4 ingredients. Add tomatoes and cook until thoroughly heated, stirring gently. Pour tomato mixture over beans and toss gently. Serve hot. Makes 8 servings.

Black-eyed Peas with Caramelized Onion & Country Ham

3 (15.8-oz.) cans packed from
  fresh shelled black-eyed peas
1 bay leaf
14-oz. can ready-to-serve
  chicken broth
2 T. olive oil
1 large red onion, diced

¼ lb. country ham, diced
½ c. balsamic vinegar
1½ t. chopped fresh thyme or
  ½ t. dried thyme
½ t. pepper
Garnish: fresh thyme sprigs

Combine first 3 ingredients in a 2-quart saucepan; bring to a boil. Cover, reduce heat and simmer 10 minutes; drain. Discard bay leaf. Return peas to pan; cover and set aside.

Meanwhile, heat oil in a large skillet over medium-high heat. Add onion; cook 5 minutes or until golden, stirring often. Reduce heat; add ham and cook 10 more minutes or until ham is crisp and onion is well browned. Stir in vinegar, chopped thyme and pepper; bring to a boil. Cook 5 minutes or until mixture is a thin syrup, stirring occasionally to loosen any caramelized bits from bottom of pan. Pour over peas; toss well. Garnish, if desired. Makes 8 servings.

Garlic-Basil Mashed Potatoes

"Mashed potatoes are a very popular comfort food at Gooseberry Patch potlucks; we're always looking for new ways to serve them! Try this recipe, we think you'll like the garlic and basil combination."
–Jo Ann

1 large garlic bulb, unpeeled
2 T. olive oil
3¼ lbs. red potatoes, peeled and
  chopped (about 9)
1 t. salt, divided

8-oz. container sour cream
½ c. grated Parmesan cheese
½ c. milk
¼ c. chopped fresh basil leaves

Cut off pointed end of garlic; place garlic on a piece of aluminum foil and drizzle with oil. Fold foil to seal. Bake at 350 degrees for 40 minutes; cool 10 minutes. Squeeze pulp from garlic cloves and mash with a fork.

Meanwhile, place potatoes and ½ teaspoon salt in a Dutch oven; cover potatoes with water and boil 25 minutes or until tender. Drain well. Return potatoes to pan. Mash potatoes; stir in garlic, ½ teaspoon salt, sour cream and Parmesan cheese. Gradually stir in milk; add basil, stirring gently.

Spoon potato mixture into a lightly greased 13"x9" baking dish. Bake, uncovered, at 350 degrees for 25 minutes or until hot and bubbly. Makes 8 to 10 servings.

Scalloped Potatoes

¼ c. butter or margarine
¼ c. all-purpose flour
2 c. milk
⅓ c. chopped green pepper
2 green onions, chopped
2-oz. jar diced pimento, drained
¾ t. salt

¼ t. ground white pepper
4 medium-size baking potatoes, peeled and thinly sliced (about 2½ lbs.)
2 c. shredded provolone cheese
⅓ c. freshly prepared French bread crumbs

This is a rich tasting potato dish that's good with any kind of roast.

Melt butter in a medium saucepan over low heat; whisk in flour until smooth. Cook one minute, whisking constantly. Gradually add milk; cook over medium heat until sauce is thickened and bubbly. Stir in green pepper and next 4 ingredients.

Layer half of potatoes in a lightly greased 13"x9" baking dish. Spoon half of sauce over potatoes; top with half of cheese. Repeat procedure.

Bake, covered, at 425 degrees for 30 minutes. Uncover and sprinkle with bread crumbs. Bake 15 more minutes or until golden. Makes 8 servings.

Vanilla-Glazed Sweet Potatoes

3 lbs. sweet potatoes, peeled
¼ c. butter or margarine
¼ c. brown sugar, packed
1 t. salt
1 t. grated orange zest

¼ t. pepper
3 T. orange juice
1 T. vanilla extract
½ c. chopped pecans, toasted

"This heavenly dish is always on our holiday table! It is rich, delicious and there are never any leftovers!"
—Teri Lindquist
Gurnee, IL

Cook sweet potatoes in boiling water to cover until tender; drain. Cool; cut into ¼-inch slices. Arrange slices, overlapping slightly, in a greased 13"x9" baking dish. Melt butter over low heat in a small saucepan. Add brown sugar and next 5 ingredients, stirring until combined and thoroughly heated (do not boil). Remove from heat and brush sauce over potato slices. Broil 6 inches from heat 6 or 7 minutes or until golden. Sprinkle with pecans. Makes 6 servings.

Roasted Vegetables

1½ lbs. sweet potatoes, peeled and cut into 1½" pieces (2 medium)
¾ lb. turnips, peeled and cut into 1½" pieces (3 small)
1 onion, peeled and cut into wedges

6 cloves garlic, peeled
3 T. olive oil
1 T. fresh rosemary, chopped
1 T. fresh oregano, chopped
1 t. salt

Roasting emphasizes the natural sweetness in vegetables. High heat creates a caramelized or crisp surface, sealing in flavor.

Combine first 5 ingredients in a large bowl; toss well. Arrange vegetables in a single layer in a large roasting pan or broiler pan. Roast at 450 degrees for 25 to 30 minutes or until well browned, stirring gently every 10 minutes. Stir in herbs and salt just before serving. Makes 6 servings.

Cornbread Dressing Croquettes

★ ★ ★

Give turkey's traditional accompaniment new interest by shaping the dressing into patties and frying them.

2 (6-oz.) pkgs. cornbread mix
3 T. butter or margarine
1 c. chopped celery
1 c. chopped onion
½ c. frozen whole kernel corn, thawed
10¾-oz. can cream of chicken soup, undiluted
¾ c. milk
¾ c. chicken broth
2 t. rubbed sage
½ t. salt
¼ t. pepper
½ c. yellow cornmeal
½ c. all-purpose flour
Vegetable oil
Garnish: celery leaves

Prepare cornbread according to package directions; cool. Crumble into a large bowl. Melt butter in a large skillet over medium-high heat; add celery, onion and corn. Cook, stirring constantly, until tender. Stir vegetables, soup, and next 5 ingredients into crumbled cornbread.

For each croquette, shape ½ cup cornbread mixture into a thick patty. Combine cornmeal and flour; roll croquettes in flour mixture. Pour oil to a depth of ¼" into a large heavy skillet. Fry croquettes in hot oil over medium-high heat until golden, turning once. Drain on paper towels. Serve hot. Garnish, if desired. Makes 16 croquettes.

Crusty Macaroni & Cheese

16-oz. pkg. large elbow macaroni
½ c. butter or margarine
½ c. all-purpose flour
4 c. milk
4 c. shredded white Cheddar
  cheese
2 t. salt
½ t. pepper
½ t. hot sauce
3 c. freshly prepared bread crumbs
6 T. butter or margarine, melted

Cook macaroni just until tender according to package directions. Drain and set aside.

Melt ½ cup butter in a heavy saucepan over low heat; whisk in flour until smooth. Cook one minute, whisking constantly. Gradually whisk in milk; cook over medium heat, whisking constantly, until mixture is thickened and bubbly. Add cheese and next 3 ingredients; stir until cheese melts. Stir in macaroni.

Spoon macaroni and cheese into a greased 13"x9" baking dish or other large baking dish. (Dish will be very full.) Toss bread crumbs with 6 tablespoons melted butter until crumbs are well coated. Sprinkle over macaroni.

Bake, uncovered, at 350 degrees for 30 minutes or until thoroughly heated and top is golden. Makes 8 to 10 servings.

★ ★ ★

Make this dish the morning of your holiday dinner; then reheat it for 5 to 10 minutes in the oven just before serving. To make fresh bread crumbs, tear a few pieces from a French baguette. Pulse in a food processor until you get coarse crumbs.

Fruited Curry Rice Bake

8¼-oz. can pear halves in juice
8-oz. can pineapple tidbits in juice
¼ c. dried apricots, chopped
¼ c. raisins
3 T. brown sugar
1 t. grated orange rind
2 (14-oz.) cans ready-to-serve
  chicken broth
2 c. converted rice, uncooked
¾ t. curry powder
½ t. salt
⅛ t. cinnamon
½ c. sliced almonds, toasted

Drain pear and pineapple, reserving juices; chop pear halves. Combine chopped pear, pineapple, apricots and next 3 ingredients in a large bowl; toss.

Add enough broth to reserved juices to measure 4 cups. Add broth mixture, rice and next 3 ingredients to fruit mixture; stir well. Pour into a lightly greased 13"x9" baking dish.

Cover and bake at 350 degrees for one hour or until liquid is absorbed and rice is tender. Let stand 5 minutes before serving. Sprinkle with almonds and serve hot. Makes 8 servings.

This dish will fill your kitchen with the rich aromas of curry and cinnamon while it cooks.

Hearty Soups & Bountiful Breads

Page 116

A brimming bowl of savory soup
is just the thing to take the nip off a
cold wintry day. Whether you're looking
for an appetizer soup or a main-dish
stew, we've got just the right selection.
Pair these soups with one of our savory
breads. But don't miss out on the
sweet breads...they're great for
breakfast, as a snack or a
"light" ending to your meal.

Sticky Bun Biscuits,
page 118

Tomato-Basil Soup

Thick and rich, this soup is just the thing to take the chill off a cold winter day.

1½ c. diced sweet onions
10 fresh basil leaves, chopped
3 cloves garlic, minced
28-oz. can whole tomatoes, undrained
2 (28-oz.) cans diced tomatoes, undrained

2 T. sugar
½ t. salt
½ t. pepper
¼ t. red pepper flakes
2 c. heavy whipping cream
Garnish: garlic croutons or fresh basil leaves

Sauté onions, basil and garlic in a Dutch oven coated with non-stick vegetable spray about 8 minutes or until onions are tender.

Process whole tomatoes in a blender or food processor 10 seconds or until smooth. Add tomato purée, diced tomatoes and sugar to onion mixture; simmer, uncovered, on low heat 2 hours. Add salt, pepper, red pepper flakes and heavy cream; cook until thoroughly heated. Garnish each serving with garlic croutons or fresh basil leaves. Makes 11 cups.

Wild Rice Soup

"For a special touch, top with crispy home-made croutons."
–Gail Saucier
Mankato, MN

3 c. chicken broth
1 c. wild rice, uncooked
1 onion, chopped
1 lb. sliced bacon, crisply cooked and crumbled, drippings reserved
2 (10¾-oz.) cans cream of potato soup

2 (4-oz.) cans sliced mushrooms, undrained
2 c. half-and-half
5-oz. jar sharp pasteurized process cheese spread
2 c. water

Bring chicken broth to a boil in a medium saucepan; stir in wild rice. Reduce heat and simmer, partially covered, 25 minutes or until rice is tender and liquid is absorbed; set aside.

Sauté onion in reserved bacon drippings in a large saucepan over medium-high heat. Stir in bacon, cream of potato soup, mushrooms, half-and-half, cheese, water and rice. Simmer until soup is thoroughly heated. Makes 12 cups.

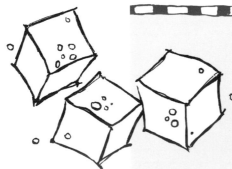

Homemade Garlic Croutons
Cut 3 slices of French bread ³⁄₄-inch thick. Spread 3 tablespoons butter over both sides of bread and sprinkle with ¼ teaspoon garlic powder. Then cut bread slices into ³⁄₄-inch cubes; place on a baking sheet and bake at 350 degrees for 15 minutes or until croutons are crisp and dry. Store in an airtight container after croutons have cooled.

Sweet Potato–Peanut Soup with Ham Croutons

¼ c. butter or margarine
1 medium onion, chopped
¾ c. chopped celery
2 cloves garlic, chopped
6 c. chicken broth
3 large sweet potatoes, peeled and coarsely chopped (about 3 lbs.)

1 T. fresh rosemary, chopped
2 c. cubed cooked ham
⅔ c. creamy peanut butter
1 c. whipping cream
¾ t. salt
¼ t. pepper
Garnish: fresh rosemary sprigs

The peanut flavor in this thick rich soup comes from creamy peanut butter. The crisp ham croutons on top are unbelieveable!

Melt butter in a Dutch oven over medium heat. Add onion, celery and garlic; sauté 10 minutes or until tender. Add broth, potatoes and chopped rosemary. Bring to a boil; cover, reduce heat and simmer 25 minutes or until potatoes are very tender.

Meanwhile, heat a large non-stick skillet over medium-high heat. Add ham and cook until browned and crisp on all sides. Drain on paper towels.

Process potato mixture, in batches, in a food processor or blender until smooth. Return potato mixture to Dutch oven; stir in peanut butter. Cook over medium-low heat until soup is smooth, stirring often. Stir in whipping cream, salt and pepper; cook until thoroughly heated.

To serve, ladle soup into individual bowls. Top each serving with ham. Garnish, if desired. Makes 10 cups.

Christmas Luncheon Crabmeat Bisque

6 T. butter, divided
1½ c. sliced mushrooms
¼ c. finely chopped green pepper
¼ c. finely chopped onion
1 scallion, chopped
2 T. fresh parsley, chopped
2 T. all-purpose flour

1 c. milk
1 t. salt
⅛ t. ground white pepper
⅛ t. hot pepper sauce
1½ c. half-and-half
1½ c. cooked crabmeat
3 T. dry sherry

Heat 4 tablespoons butter in a large skillet. Add mushrooms, green pepper, onion, scallion and parsley; sauté 5 minutes or until vegetables are tender.

Heat remaining 2 tablespoons butter in a saucepan; stir in flour. Add milk and cook, stirring until thickened and smooth. Stir in salt, pepper and hot pepper sauce. Add sautéed vegetables and half-and-half. Bring to a boil, stirring constantly. Reduce heat to low; add crabmeat and simmer, uncovered, for 5 minutes. Stir in sherry just before serving. Makes 4 servings.

Seafood Gumbo

★ ★ ★

Get this gumbo started in a skillet (for cooking bacon and then a roux); then pour it all in a slow cooker to simmer several hours and develop rich flavor. Add the seafood the last hour so it doesn't get overcooked.

12-oz. pkg. bacon
6 T. all-purpose flour
1 large onion, chopped
1¼ c. chopped celery
1 large green pepper, chopped
3 cloves garlic, minced
16-oz. pkg. frozen sliced okra, thawed
14½-oz. can diced tomatoes, undrained
14-oz. can chicken broth
8-oz. bottle clam juice

⅓ c. fresh parsley, chopped
2 bay leaves
2¼ t. Creole seasoning
½ t. salt
1 lb. unpeeled large fresh shrimp, peeled
12-oz. container fresh oysters, drained
½ lb. fresh lump crabmeat, drained
Hot cooked rice
Filé powder (optional)

Cut bacon into one-inch pieces. Cook bacon in a large skillet over medium heat until crisp; remove bacon and drain on paper towels, reserving drippings in skillet. (Cover and chill bacon until gumbo is done.) Whisk flour into drippings and cook over medium heat, whisking constantly, until roux is caramel-colored (about 15 minutes). Add onion and next 3 ingredients; cook until vegetables are crisp-tender, stirring constantly.

Transfer vegetable mixture to a 4-quart electric slow cooker. Stir in okra and next 7 ingredients. Cover and cook on low heat 6 hours. Add shrimp, oysters and crabmeat; cover and cook on high heat one hour or until shrimp turn pink and edges of oysters begin to curl. Discard bay leaves.

To serve, ladle gumbo over rice into individual bowls. (Microwave bacon one minute to reheat.) Sprinkle each serving with bacon. Serve with filé powder, if desired. Makes 12 cups.

Chicken Cacciatore Stew

2 T. olive oil
4 chicken leg-thigh combinations,
 skinned and separated
1 large onion, chopped
3 carrots, sliced
1 large green pepper, chopped
2 cloves garlic, minced
8-oz. pkg. sliced mushrooms
32-oz. carton chicken broth
2 (14½-oz.) cans diced tomatoes
 with roasted garlic, undrained

1 c. water
½ c. white wine or chicken broth
⅓ c. fresh oregano leaves
3 T. fresh thyme leaves
½ t. salt
½ t. pepper
3 bay leaves
4 oz. uncooked spaghetti, broken
 into 3-inch pieces
Freshly shredded Parmesan cheese

Mushrooms, onions, tomatoes and wine typify cacciatore. Taste them all in this chicken stew enhanced with pasta and fragrant herbs. Add a salad and your meal's complete.

Pour oil into a large Dutch oven. Brown chicken in hot oil over medium-high heat 4 minutes on each side; transfer chicken to a platter.

Sauté onion, carrots, green pepper and garlic in Dutch oven 5 minutes or until tender. Add mushrooms; cook 3 minutes, stirring often. Add chicken, chicken broth and next 8 ingredients. Bring to a boil; cover, reduce heat and simmer 30 minutes. Add spaghetti and cook, covered, 12 more minutes. Discard bay leaves. Sprinkle stew with Parmesan cheese. Makes 12½ cups.

Ham & Lentil Stew

2 leeks
1 meaty ham bone from a spiral
 sliced ham
4 carrots, sliced into ½-inch pieces
½ green pepper, chopped
1 c. dried lentils
⅓ c. fresh parsley, chopped
14½-oz. can diced tomatoes with
 green pepper and onion,
 undrained

14-oz. can ready-to-serve beef
 broth
10½-oz. can beef consommé
1½ c. water
¼ t. pepper

This hearty stew can be cooked in a slow cooker or on the stove-top. For the stovetop, combine all ingredients in a large Dutch oven. Bring to a boil; cover, reduce heat and sim-mer 1½ hours. Remove ham bone, cut off meat and continue as directed in recipe.

Remove root, tough outer layers and tops from leeks, leaving 2 inches of dark leaves. Slice leeks; rinse well and drain.

Place ham bone in a 5-quart electric slow cooker. Add leeks, carrots and remaining ingredients. Cook, covered, on high heat one hour; reduce heat to low heat and cook 6 hours. Remove ham bone; cool slightly. Cut off meat and chop. Discard bone; return to meat to stew. Makes 10 cups.

Chipotle Chili con Carne

This is no ordinary chili. Beef, venison and pork mingle with smoky chipotle peppers for a thick, spicy concoction. Use all of one type of meat, if desired, and just one chipotle pepper for a milder version.

1 lb. ground round
1 lb. ground venison
16-oz. pkg. sage-flavored pork sausage
1 medium onion, chopped
1 large green pepper, chopped
2 cloves garlic, minced
2 (14½-oz.) cans diced tomatoes, undrained
15-oz. can tomato sauce

2 chipotle peppers in adobo sauce, seeded and chopped
2 t. adobo sauce
1 T. chili powder
2 t. dried oregano
1 t. cumin
½ t. salt
Shredded Monterey Jack cheese
Sour cream
Sliced green onions

Cook first 6 ingredients in a large skillet over medium-high heat, stirring until meat crumbles and is no longer pink.

Meanwhile, stir together diced tomatoes and next 7 ingredients in a 4½-quart electric slow cooker. Drain meat mixture and stir into tomato mixture. Cover and cook on low heat 5 hours.

To serve, spoon chili into bowls. Top with cheese, sour cream and green onions. Makes 9 cups.

Fireside Chili

1½ lbs. ground beef
1 c. chopped green pepper
1 c. chopped onions
2 (15-oz.) cans red kidney beans, drained
28-oz. can tomatoes, chopped and undrained
15-oz. can tomato sauce
1½ c. water

2 T. chili powder
2 T. Worcestershire sauce
1 T. honey
1 t. salt
½ t. dried basil
½ t. cinnamon
¼ t. allspice
1 large bay leaf

Cook ground beef, green pepper and onion in a Dutch oven, stirring until meat crumbles and is no longer pink; drain. Add kidney beans and remaining ingredients. Simmer, covered, 1½ hours, stirring occasionally. Discard bay leaf. Makes 11 cups.

Spicy Pepperoni Biscuits

2 c. all-purpose flour
1 T. baking powder
½ t. salt
½ t. dry mustard

¼ t. ground red pepper
⅓ c. shortening
½ c. finely chopped pepperoni
¾ c. milk

Combine first 5 ingredients; cut in shortening with a pastry blender or 2 knives until mixture is crumbly. Stir in pepperoni. Add milk, stirring just until dry ingredients are moistened.

Turn dough out onto a lightly floured surface; knead 3 or 4 times. Roll dough to ½-inch thickness; cut dough with a 2-inch or 2½-inch biscuit cutter and place biscuits on a lightly greased baking sheet. Bake at 425 degrees for 13 to 15 minutes or until lightly browned. Makes one dozen.

"Every Thanksgiving for the last 17 years, our family has vacationed or gathered at home together. Fireside Chili is usually cooking while the adults are catching up on family events and the children are running around! Whenever this chili is served, it will always remind me of these special family times together."
–Dorothy Jackson
Weddington, NC

Serve these warm biscuits for brunch with mugs of hot soup.

Sticky Bun Biscuits

(pictured on page 111)

(pictured on page 111)

For the ultimate break-fast, add coffee and fresh fruit.

1 c. brown sugar, packed
¾ c. butter or margarine
½ c. light corn syrup
1 c. coarsely chopped pecans

3 c. self-rising flour
¼ c. sugar
¾ c. shortening
1 c. milk

Combine first 3 ingredients in a saucepan; cook over medium heat, stirring constantly, until melted and smooth. Pour mixture into a greased 13"x9" pan; sprinkle with pecans. Set aside.

Combine flour and ¼ cup sugar; cut in shortening with a pastry blender or 2 knives until mixture is crumbly. Add milk, stirring until dry ingredients are moistened. Turn dough out onto a lightly floured surface; knead 4 or 5 times.

Roll dough to ¾-inch thickness; cut with a 2-inch biscuit cutter. Place biscuits over brown sugar mixture in pan. Bake at 400 degrees for 18 to 20 minutes or until done. Remove from oven and let stand 5 minutes. Invert onto a serving platter; remove pan. Spoon any additional brown sugar glaze over biscuits; serve immediately. Makes 1½ dozen.

Elf Muffins

(pictured on opposite page)

(pictured on opposite page)

To make larger muffins, spoon batter into regular-size muffin pans and bake at 400 degrees for 20 minutes or until golden. Makes 10 muffins. Whoever gets the muffin with the almond is favored by Santa for sure!

1½ c. all-purpose flour
2 t. baking powder
½ t. salt
½ t. nutmeg
½ c. sugar
⅓ c. shortening
1 egg

⅓ c. milk
1 t. vanilla extract
1 t. almond extract
1½ c. peeled and shredded Granny
   Smith apple
1 almond
Topping

Combine first 4 ingredients in a large bowl; make a well in center of mixture. Beat sugar and shortening at medium speed with an electric mixer until creamy. Add egg and milk, beating well. Add to dry ingredients, stirring just until moistened. Add flavorings; stir in apple. Place one almond into one muffin cup. Spoon batter into greased miniature (1¾") muffin pans, filling ⅔ full.

Bake at 400 degrees for 15 minutes or until golden. Remove from pan immediately and cool slightly on a wire rack. Dip muffins into Topping. Makes 32 muffins.

Topping

½ c. butter, melted
⅓ c. sugar

¾ t. cinnamon

Stir together all ingredients in a small bowl. Let cool. Makes ½ cup.

Cheddar Scones

These light-textured little wedges of cheese bread are ideal for dunking into a steaming bowl of chili. They're also good for breakfast.

1¾ c. all-purpose flour
1 T. sugar
2 t. baking powder
¾ t. salt
¼ c. cold butter, cut into pieces

1 c. finely shredded sharp Cheddar cheese
1 egg, lightly beaten
⅔ c. half-and-half
1 T. butter, melted

Combine first 4 ingredients in a large bowl; cut in ¼ cup cold butter with a pastry blender or 2 knives until mixture is crumbly. Stir in cheese.

Stir together egg and half-and-half. Gradually add to flour mixture, stirring with a fork just until dry ingredients are moistened. Turn dough out onto a lightly floured surface and knead 3 or 4 times. Gently roll into a ball.

Pat dough into a 7-inch circle on an ungreased baking sheet. Cut into 6 wedges, using a sharp knife. (Do not separate wedges.)

Bake at 400 degrees for 16 to 18 minutes or until golden. Remove from oven; brush with one tablespoon melted butter. Serve warm. Makes 6 scones.

Eggnog Tea Bread

16-oz. pkg. pound cake mix
¾ c. refrigerated eggnog
½ t. nutmeg

2 eggs
1 c. sifted powdered sugar
1 T. refrigerated eggnog

Combine first 4 ingredients in a large mixing bowl; beat at medium speed with an electric mixer 3 minutes. Pour batter into 4 greased 6"x3" loaf pans. Bake at 350 degrees for 30 minutes or until a toothpick inserted in center comes out clean. Remove from pans; cool on wire racks.

Combine powdered sugar and one tablespoon eggnog, stirring well; drizzle over bread. Makes 4 loaves.

Use your extra eggnog to make this sweet bread that makes enough little loaves for you and three friends.

Buttery Dinner Rolls

¼-oz. pkg. active dry yeast
½ c. sugar
1 c. warm milk (100 degrees to 110 degrees)

4½ c. all-purpose flour
2 eggs, lightly beaten
½ c. butter, melted
1 t. salt

Combine first 3 ingredients in a 2-cup measuring cup; let yeast mixture stand 5 minutes.

Combine flour and remaining 3 ingredients in a bowl; stir in yeast mixture until a soft dough forms. Turn dough out onto a lightly floured surface and knead for 5 to 10 minutes or until smooth and elastic. Place in a well-greased bowl, turning to grease top.

Cover and let rise in a warm place (85 degrees), free from drafts, 1½ hours or until double in bulk. Punch dough down and divide into 2 equal portions. Roll each portion into a 9-inch circle and cut each circle into 8 wedges. Roll up each wedge, starting at the wide end of the wedge. Place rolls, point side down, on lightly greased baking sheets; curve ends slightly inward.

Cover and let rise in a warm place, free from drafts, 45 minutes or until double in bulk. Bake at 375 degrees for 16 minutes or until tops are golden brown. Makes 16 rolls.

"A County Fair Blue Ribbon Winner. . .so easy for busy days!"
—Clara Hilton
Marengo, OH

Amish Orange Rolls

1 c. shortening
⅔ c. sugar
1½ t. salt
2 c. warm milk (120 degrees to 130 degrees)
4 (¼-oz). pkgs. active dry yeast
1 c. warm water (100 degrees to 110 degrees)

4 eggs, lightly beaten
5 t. grated orange rind
½ c. fresh orange juice
12 c. all-purpose flour, divided
3 T. melted butter

Combine shortening, sugar and salt in a large bowl. Stir in milk; set aside.
Combine yeast and warm water in a 2-cup measuring cup; let stand 5 minutes.
Stir yeast mixture, eggs, orange rind and orange juice into shortening mixture. Stir in 9 cups flour. Turn dough out onto a well-floured surface; knead in remaining 3 cups flour to make a soft dough. Knead until smooth and elastic (about 8 minutes). Place in a well-greased bowl, turning to grease top.
Cover and let rise in a warm place (85 degrees), free from drafts, 45 minutes or until double in bulk.
Punch dough down and roll dough to one-inch thickness; cut with a 3-inch round cutter. Place in 3 lightly greased 13"x9" pans. Cover and let rise in a warm place, free from drafts, 30 minutes or until double in bulk.
Bake at 350 degrees for 20 minutes or until golden. Remove rolls from pans; brush with melted butter. Cool on wire racks 10 minutes. Drizzle with Orange Icing. Makes 3 dozen.

Orange Icing

3 c. sifted powdered sugar
1 t. grated orange rind

¼ c. plus 1 t. fresh orange juice

Combine all ingredients in a bowl and stir until smooth. Makes one cup.

Cream Cheese Braids

16-oz. pkg. hot rolls mix
8-oz. pkg. cream cheese, softened
⅓ c. sugar
1 t. vanilla extract
1 egg yolk

⅛ t. salt
1 egg yolk, lightly beaten
1 c. sifted powdered sugar
1 T. milk
1 t. vanilla extract

The perfect food for Christmas morning...beautiful braided bread drizzled with icing.

Prepare dough from hot roll mix according to package directions, using yeast packet. Turn dough out onto a lightly floured surface and knead 4 to 5 times. Divide dough in half; roll each portion of dough to a 12"x8" rectangle.

Process cream cheese and next 4 ingredients in a food processor or electric mixer until blended. Spread half of cream cheese mixture lengthwise down center of each dough rectangle.

Working with one dough rectangle at a time, cut 9 (3-inch) deep slits into each long side of dough. Fold strips over cream cheese filling, alternating sides and making a braid. Pinch ends to seal and tuck under, if desired. Carefully place loaves on greased baking sheets.

Cover and let rise in a warm place (85 degrees), free from drafts, 30 minutes. Brush tops with beaten egg yolk. Bake at 375 degrees for 15 minutes or until golden.

Combine powdered sugar, milk, and one teaspoon vanilla, stirring well; drizzle over warm loaves. Makes 2 (12-inch) loaves.

Visions of Sugarplums

Page 130

Tie your apron strings, turn

on the oven and bake some sweets to

share with your loved ones.

Try our chocolatey cakes, fruity

cobblers, coffee cakes, pies or

Christmas cookies galore.

You'll want to lick the bowl clean and

your kitchen will smell

wonderful, too!

Heavenly Chocolate
Chunk Cookies, page 137

Three-Layer Chocolate Cake

1 c. butter, softened
1¾ c. sugar
3 eggs
2¼ c. all-purpose flour
1½ t. baking powder
1 t. baking soda
¼ t. salt
1 c. baking cocoa
1¾ c. milk
1 T. vanilla extract
Fudge Frosting

Beat butter at medium speed with an electric mixer about 2 minutes or until creamy. Gradually add sugar, beating 5 to 7 minutes. Add eggs, one at a time, beating just until yellow disappears.

Combine flour and next 4 ingredients in a large bowl; add to butter mixture alternately with milk, beginning and ending with flour mixture. Beat at low speed just until blended after each addition. Stir in vanilla. Pour batter into 3 greased and floured 9" cake pans.

Bake at 350 degrees for 22 minutes or until a toothpick inserted in center comes out clean. Cool in pans on wire racks 10 minutes. Remove from pans and cool completely on wire racks.

Spread ¾ cup Fudge Frosting between layers and spread remaining Fudge Frosting on top and sides. Makes 12 servings.

Fudge Frosting

1 c. butter, softened
4 c. powdered sugar
½ c. baking cocoa
2 t. vanilla extract
5 T. milk

Combine all ingredients in a mixing bowl. Beat at medium speed with an electric mixer until smooth. Makes 3½ cups.

Carrot-Praline Cake

(pictured on page 2)

Buttery bits of home-made pecan praline dot each layer of this moist carrot cake.

1 T. butter
3 T. sugar
½ c. chopped pecans
1¼ c. sugar
¾ c. vegetable oil
1 t. vanilla extract
3 eggs
2 c. all-purpose flour
1¼ t. baking soda
¼ t. salt
½ t. cinnamon
1 (8-oz.) can crushed pineapple in juice, undrained
2 c. shredded carrot
1 (8-oz.) pkg. cream cheese, softened
¼ c. butter, softened
¼ c. brown sugar, packed
1 t. vanilla extract
3 c. powdered sugar
1 c. chopped pecans
1 (8-oz.) can pineapple tidbits in syrup, drained
Garnish: Pecan halves

Melt 1 tablespoon butter in a skillet; add 3 tablespoons sugar, and cook over low heat until mixture bubbles. Stir in 1/2 cup pecans; cook until pecans are coated and sugar begins to caramelize. Pour onto a sheet of wax paper; cool. Break into small pieces.

Beat 1 1/4 cups sugar, oil and 1 teaspoon vanilla at medium speed with an electric mixer one minute. Add eggs, one at a time; beat until blended after each addition.

Combine flour and next 3 ingredients; add to oil mixture, beating at low speed until blended after each addition. Stir in crushed pineapple, carrot, and praline pieces. Pour into 2 greased and floured 9" round cake pans.

Bake at 350 degrees for 30 minutes or until a toothpick inserted in center comes out clean. Cool in pans on wire racks 10 minutes. Remove from pans and cool completely on wire racks.

Beat cream cheese and 1/4 cup softened butter at medium speed until creamy; gradually add brown sugar and one teaspoon vanilla, beating well. Add powdered sugar, 1/2 cup at a time, beating well after each addition. Spread frosting between layers and on top and sides of cake. Press one cup chopped pecans into frosting on sides of cake. Press pineapple tidbits into frosting around top edge of cake. Garnish, if desired. Makes 10 servings.

Cranberry Coffee Cake
(pictured on cover)

★ ★ ★

1/2 c. butter or margarine, softened
1 c. sugar
2 eggs
2 c. all-purpose flour
1 t. baking soda
1 t. baking powder
1/2 t. salt

8-oz. container sour cream
1 t. almond extract
3/4 c. whole berry cranberry sauce
1/2 c. chopped pecans
3/4 c. powdered sugar
2 1/2 t. water
1/2 t. almond extract

To get a pretty swirl in this coffee cake, take extra care when spooning cranberry sauce over the batter. You want to be sure the thick sauce rests on top of the batter.

Cream butter and sugar at medium speed with an electric mixer. Add eggs, one at a time, beating well after each addition.

Combine flour, baking soda, baking powder and salt. Add to butter mixture alternately with sour cream, beating until mixture is smooth; stir in almond extract.

Pour 2/3 of batter into a lightly greased and floured 10" tube pan. Spoon cranberry sauce over batter. Spoon remaining batter on top of cranberry sauce. Sprinkle with chopped pecans.

Bake at 350 degrees for 40 to 45 minutes or until a long toothpick inserted in center comes out clean. Cool in pan 10 to 15 minutes. Remove from pan and cool completely on a wire rack.

Combine powdered sugar, water and almond extract; drizzle over cake. Makes 12 to 15 servings.

Chocolate-Peppermint Bundt® Cake

(pictured on page 56)

(pictured on page 56)

Devil's food cake mix gives you a jump start with this dessert, and chocolate pudding and sour cream make each bite moist.

18¼-oz. pkg. devil's food cake mix
½ c. sugar
3.9-oz. pkg. chocolate instant
   pudding mix
1 c. vegetable oil
4 eggs

8-oz. container sour cream
1 t. peppermint extract
1 c. powdered sugar
1½ to 2 T. milk
½ c. coarsely crushed hard
   peppermint candies

Heavily grease and flour a 12-cup Bundt® pan. Set aside.

Combine first 7 ingredients in a large mixing bowl. Beat at low speed with an electric mixer just until combined. Beat at high speed 2 minutes. Pour batter into prepared pan.

Bake at 350 degrees for 50 minutes or until a long toothpick inserted in center comes out clean. Cool in pan on a wire rack 15 minutes; remove from pan and cool completely on wire rack. Place cake on a serving plate. Stir together powdered sugar and enough milk to make a drizzling consistency. Drizzle glaze over cake; sprinkle with crushed candies. Makes 12 servings.

Cranberry-Ginger Crumble Cake

(pictured on page 5)

(pictured on page 5)

A pretty cranberry filling and a yummy candied ginger topping will keep you nibbling on this coffee cake.

2 c. fresh or frozen cranberries
1½ c. sugar
1 T. cornstarch
1½ t. grated lemon rind
¾ c. water
¾ c. all-purpose flour
¼ c. sugar
¼ c. cold butter, cut into pieces
2.7-oz. jar crystallized ginger,
   finely chopped (½ cup)

8-oz. pkg. cream cheese, softened
½ c. butter or margarine, softened
¾ c. sugar
2 eggs
2 c. all-purpose flour
1½ t. baking powder
½ t. baking soda
½ t. salt
¼ c. milk
½ t. vanilla extract

Stir together first 4 ingredients in a saucepan; stir in water. Bring to a boil; reduce heat and simmer, uncovered, 25 minutes or until cranberry skins pop and mixture is thickened. Remove from heat; set aside to cool.

Combine ¾ cup flour, ¼ cup sugar and ¼ cup butter with a pastry blender or 2 knives until crumbly. Stir in ginger; set aside.

Beat cream cheese and ½ cup butter at medium speed with an electric mixer until creamy; gradually add ¾ cup sugar, beating well. Add eggs, one at a time, beating until blended after each addition.

Combine 2 cups flour and next 3 ingredients; add to cream cheese mixture alternately with milk, beginning and ending with flour mixture. Beat at low speed until blended after each addition. Stir in vanilla. Spoon half of batter into a greased 13"x9" pan. Spread reserved cranberry mixture over batter. Drop remaining batter by rounded tablespoonfuls over cranberry mixture. Sprinkle with ginger topping.

Bake at 350 degrees for 32 to 35 minutes or until toothpick inserted in center comes out clean. Cool in pan on a wire rack. Makes 12 servings.

Carrot Cake Roulage

4 eggs
½ c. water
18¼-oz. pkg. spice cake mix
1 c. grated carrot
3 T. powdered sugar, divided
15¼-oz. can crushed pineapple in
  heavy syrup

2 (16-oz.) cans cream cheese
  frosting
½ c. chopped pecans, toasted
Powdered sugar
Garnish: toasted chopped pecans

Carrot cake takes a new shape in this jelly roll. Look for the rich cream cheese frosting rolled up inside.

Coat two 15"x10" jelly roll pans with non-stick vegetable spray; line with wax paper and coat wax paper with vegetable spray. Set aside.

Beat eggs in a large bowl at medium-high speed with an electric mixer 5 minutes. Add water, beating at low speed until blended. Gradually add cake mix, beating at low speed until moistened. Beat mixture at medium-high speed 2 minutes. Fold in grated carrot.

Spread batter evenly in prepared pans (layers will be thin). Bake, one at a time or in separate ovens, at 350 degrees on the middle rack 13 minutes or until each cake springs back when lightly touched in center.

Sift 1½ tablespoons powdered sugar in a 15"x10" rectangle on a cloth towel; repeat with remaining 1½ tablespoons powdered sugar and a second towel. When cakes are done, immediately loosen from sides of pan and turn each out onto a sugared towel. Peel off wax paper. Starting at narrow end, roll up each cake and towel together; place, seam side down, on wire racks to cool.

Drain pineapple, reserving ¼ cup syrup. Press pineapple between paper towels to remove excess moisture. Combine pineapple, cream cheese frosting, and ½ cup pecans; stir well.

Unroll cakes; brush each lightly with 2 tablespoons reserved pineapple syrup. Spread each cake with half of frosting mixture. Reroll cakes without towels; place, seam side down, on serving plates.

Cover and chill at least one hour. Dust cakes with additional powdered sugar before serving. Garnish, if desired. Makes 2 cake rolls (24 servings).

Bourbon-Chocolate Pecan Pie

★ ★ ★

This decadent chocolate pecan pie is every bit as good if you make it without bourbon.

½ (15-oz.) pkg. refrigerated pie crusts
4 eggs
1 c. light corn syrup
6 T. butter or margarine, melted
½ c. sugar
¼ c. brown sugar, packed

3 T. bourbon (optional)
1 T. all-purpose flour
1 T. vanilla extract
1 c. coarsely chopped pecans
1 c. semi-sweet chocolate chips, melted

Fit pie crust into a lightly greased 9" pie plate according to package directions, being careful to press together any cracks. Fold edges under and crimp.

Whisk together eggs and next 7 ingredients until blended; stir in pecans and melted chocolate. Pour filling into pie crust.

Bake on lowest oven rack at 350 degrees for one hour or until set, shielding pie with aluminum foil after 20 minutes. Cool completely on a wire rack. Makes 8 servings.

Macaroon Tartlets

1 c. butter, softened
1 c. sugar, divided
3 eggs, divided
1 t. vanilla extract

2 c. all-purpose flour
1 lb. almond paste
½ t. almond extract
½ c. slivered almonds

These buttery mini tarts have a soft almond paste filling.

Beat butter at medium speed with an electric mixer until creamy; gradually add ½ cup sugar, beating well. Add one egg and vanilla; beat well. Gradually add flour; beat well.

Shape dough into 48 (one-inch) balls; press balls into lightly greased miniature (1¾") muffin pans, pressing evenly into bottom and up sides. Set aside.

Beat almond paste at medium speed until creamy; gradually add remaining ½ cup sugar, beating well.

Add almond extract and remaining 2 eggs, beating well. Spoon mixture into prepared shells. Top each tartlet with 3 slivered almonds. Bake at 325 degrees for 25 minutes or until golden. Cool in pans on wire racks 10 minutes; remove to wire racks and cool completely. Makes 4 dozen.

Caramel Apple Crisp

½ c. all-purpose flour
½ c. sugar
½ t. cinnamon
¼ t. nutmeg
40 caramels, quartered
9 c. peeled and sliced Granny
    Smith or other cooking apples
    (about 2½ lbs.)

¼ c. orange juice
½ c. sugar
⅓ c. all-purpose flour
¼ c. butter, cut into pieces
⅔ c. quick-cooking oats, uncooked
½ c. chopped walnuts

Let your kids help unwrap caramels for this fruit dessert.

Combine first 4 ingredients in a large bowl; add caramels and stir to coat.

Toss sliced apples with orange juice in another bowl; add to caramel mixture and combine well. Spoon apple mixture into a lightly greased 13"x9" baking dish.

Combine ½ cup sugar and ⅓ cup flour in a small bowl; cut in butter with a pastry blender or 2 knives until mixture is crumbly. Stir in oats and walnuts; sprinkle topping mixture over apples. Bake at 350 degrees for one hour or until apples are tender. Makes 15 to 20 servings.

Gingerbread Trifle

½ c. butter or margarine, softened
½ c. brown sugar, packed
1 egg
1 c. molasses
2½ c. all-purpose flour
1 T. ground ginger
2 t. baking powder
½ t. baking soda

½ t. salt
1 c. hot water
Custard
8-oz. container frozen whipped
  topping, thawed
4 (1.4-oz.) English toffee-flavored
  candy bars, coarsely chopped

Layer old-fashioned gingerbread with home-made vanilla custard, and you get this yummy dessert that can be made ahead.

Beat butter at medium speed with an electric mixer until creamy. Gradually add sugar, beating until light and fluffy. Add egg and molasses, mixing well.

Combine flour and next 4 ingredients; add to butter mixture alternately with water, beginning and ending with flour mixture. Beat at low speed after each addition until blended. Pour batter into a greased 13"x9" pan.

Bake at 350 degrees for 30 to 35 minutes or until a toothpick inserted in center comes out clean. Cool in pan on a wire rack.

Cut gingerbread into cubes. Arrange ⅓ of gingerbread cubes in a 3-quart trifle bowl; top with ⅓ of Custard. Repeat layers twice, ending with Custard. Cover and chill until ready to serve.

Before serving, spread whipped topping over trifle. Sprinkle with chopped candy bars. Makes 10 servings.

Custard

1⅓ c. sugar
⅔ c. all-purpose flour
½ t. salt

5 c. milk
6 egg yolks, lightly beaten
1 T. vanilla extract

Combine first 3 ingredients in a large heavy saucepan; whisk in milk. Cook over medium heat, stirring constantly, until thickened and bubbly. Gradually stir about ¼ of hot mixture into egg yolks; add to remaining hot mixture, stirring constantly. Cook over medium heat, stirring constantly 3 minutes. Remove from heat; add vanilla. Cool to room temperature. Assemble trifle, or cover and chill custard until ready for assembly. Makes 5 cups.

Easy as Pie
•Cut extra pastry with leaf-shape cutters or Christmas cookie cutters for a quick & easy way to decorate the top of a pie. Just brush bottom of pastry cutouts with water and stick onto pie crust before baking.
•Use a pizza cutter to make pastry strips for a lattice design. Braid pastry strips on a large baking sheet; freeze briefly and then flip lattice over onto top of pie before baking.
•Brush pie crust with a beaten egg before baking to give the crust golden color and shine.
•Sprinkle sugar or cinnamon sugar onto unbaked pie to give some sparkle and a little crunch.

Gingerbread Fruitcake Cookies

★ ★ ★

14-oz. pkg. gingerbread mix
¼ c. plus 2 T. water
¼ c. butter or margarine, melted
4-oz. container candied orange
  peel, chopped
½ c. golden raisins
½ c. chopped pecans
1½ c. powdered sugar
2½ T. lemon juice or orange juice

These little drop cookies have a big punch of ginger flavor.

Combine first 3 ingredients, stirring until smooth. Fold in candied orange peel, raisins and pecans.

Drop dough by rounded teaspoonfuls onto lightly greased baking sheets.

Bake at 350 degrees for 10 minutes. Let cool slightly on baking sheets. Remove to wire racks and let cool completely.

Combine powdered sugar and lemon juice, stirring until smooth. Drizzle over cooled cookies. Makes 4 dozen.

Christmas Crinkles

(pictured on page 41)

4-oz. bar white chocolate, coarsely
  chopped
⅓ c. butter or margarine,
  softened
1½ c. sugar, divided
¼ c. buttermilk
1 t. vanilla extract
1 egg
2½ c. all-purpose flour
½ t. baking soda
¼ t. salt
½ c. semi-sweet chocolate chips
1 T. shortening
Crushed hard peppermint candy

Melt white chocolate in a saucepan over low heat, stirring constantly. Remove from heat. Beat butter at medium speed with an electric mixer until creamy. Gradually add one cup sugar; beat well. Add melted white chocolate, buttermilk, vanilla and egg; beat well.

Combine flour, soda and salt; gradually add to batter, beating well. Cover and chill one hour.

Shape dough into one-inch balls; roll balls in remaining ½ cup sugar. Place 2 inches apart on ungreased baking sheets. Bake at 375 degrees for 8 minutes or until bottoms of cookies are lightly browned. Cool slightly on baking sheets. Remove to wire racks to cool completely.

Melt chocolate chips and shortening in a saucepan over low heat, stirring constantly. Drizzle over cookies; sprinkle with crushed candy. Makes 5 dozen.

Chocolate-Caramel Thumbprints

½ c. butter or margarine, softened
½ c. sugar
2 (1-oz.) squares semi-sweet
    baking chocolate, melted
1 egg yolk
2 t. vanilla extract
1¼ c. all-purpose flour

1 t. baking soda
¼ t. salt
¾ c. very finely chopped pecans
16 milk caramels
2½ T. whipping cream
⅔ c. semi-sweet chocolate chips
2 t. shortening

A gooey caramel center guarantees these cookies will disappear quickly!

Beat butter at medium speed with an electric mixer until creamy; gradually add sugar, beating well. Add melted chocolate and egg yolk, beating until blended. Stir in vanilla. Combine flour, soda and salt; add to butter mixture, beating well. Cover and chill one hour.

Shape dough into one-inch balls; roll balls in chopped pecans. Place balls one-inch apart on greased baking sheets. Press thumb gently into center of each ball, leaving a thumbprint.

Bake at 350 degrees for 12 minutes or until set. Meanwhile, combine caramels and whipping cream in top of a double boiler over simmering water. Cook over medium-low heat, stirring constantly, until caramels melt and mixture is smooth.

Remove cookies from oven; cool slightly and press center of each cookie again. Quickly spoon ¾ teaspoon caramel mixture into center of each cookie. Remove cookies to wire racks to cool.

Place chocolate chips and shortening in a heavy-duty, plastic zipping bag; seal bag. Microwave on high power (100%) one to 1½ minutes; squeeze bag until chocolate melts. Snip a tiny hole in one corner of bag, using scissors. Drizzle chocolate over cooled cookies. Makes about 2½ dozen.

Rolled Cinnamon-Sugar Angels

¾ c. unsalted butter, softened
1 c. sugar
1 egg
1 t. vanilla extract
3 c. all-purpose flour
2 t. baking powder

½ t. baking soda
½ t. cinnamon
¼ t. salt
15-oz. container creamy vanilla
    frosting

This cinnamon dough deserves its celestial shape but works fine with any favorite cookie cutters you have on hand.

Beat butter at medium speed with an electric mixer until fluffy; gradually add sugar, beating well. Add egg and vanilla, beating well. Combine flour and next 4 ingredients; gradually add to butter mixture, beating until blended. Shape dough into a ball. Cover and chill 30 minutes.

Roll dough to ⅛-inch thickness on a lightly floured surface. Cut with 3-inch angel-shaped cookie cutters and gently transfer to lightly greased baking sheets (dough is fragile). Bake at 375 degrees for 6 to 7 minutes or until lightly browned. Carefully remove cookies to wire racks to cool.

Place frosting in a microwave-safe bowl. Microwave, uncovered, at high power (100%) 45 seconds or just until pourable; spoon frosting on top of cookies. Let stand on wire racks until dry. Makes 3 dozen.

Peanut Butter Shortbread

¾ c. butter, softened
½ c. creamy peanut butter
½ c. brown sugar, packed

¼ t. vanilla extract
2¼ c. all-purpose flour
¼ t. salt

Creamy peanut butter adds a tasty new dimension to this butter cookie.

Beat butter and peanut butter at medium speed with an electric mixer until creamy; gradually add sugar, beating well. Stir in vanilla.

Combine flour and salt; gradually add to butter mixture, beating at low speed until blended.

Roll dough to ½-inch thickness on a lightly floured surface. Cut with a 2½-inch round cutter or Christmas cookie cutter. Place 2 inches apart on ungreased baking sheets.

Bake at 275 degrees for 45 minutes. Cool 2 minutes on baking sheets. Remove to wire racks to cool. Makes 15 cookies.

Peanut Butter-Chocolate Chip Shortbread: *Stir ½ cup miniature semi-sweet chocolate chips into the dough before rolling, cutting and baking.*

Aunt Neal's Old-Fashioned Tea Cakes

"These delicious tea cakes were made by my Aunt Cornelia ('Neal') on special occasions and holidays, using homemade hand-churned butter and eggs she gathered from the henhouse. This southern Georgia version dates back to the turn of the twentieth century."
—Ana Kelly
Birmingham, AL

1 c. butter, softened
1 c. sugar
1 egg, lightly beaten
1 t. vanilla extract
3 c. all-purpose flour

1 t. baking powder
½ t. baking soda
½ t. salt
½ c. milk
Sparkling white sugar

Beat butter at medium speed with an electric mixer until creamy; gradually add one cup sugar, beating well. Add egg and vanilla; beat well.

Combine flour and next 3 ingredients; add to butter mixture alternately with milk, beginning and ending with flour mixture. Mix at low speed after each addition just until blended. Shape dough into 2 discs. Wrap in wax paper and chill at least one hour.

Roll each disc to ¼-inch thickness on a floured surface. Cut with a 3½-inch round cutter; place one inch apart on lightly greased baking sheets. Sprinkle with sparkling sugar. Bake at 400 degrees for 7 to 8 minutes or until edges are lightly browned. Cool one minute on baking sheets; remove to wire racks to cool. Makes 2 dozen.

Heavenly Chocolate Chunk Cookies

(pictured on page 125)

2 c. plus 2 T. all-purpose flour
½ t. baking soda
½ t. salt
¾ c. butter or margarine
2 T. instant coffee granules
1 c. brown sugar, packed
½ c. sugar

1 egg
1 egg yolk
11½-oz. pkg. semi-sweet double
   chocolate mega-chips or 12-oz.
   pkg. semi-sweet chocolate chips
1 c. walnut halves, toasted

There's a big chocolate taste in every bite of these deluxe chocolate chip cookies.

Combine first 3 ingredients; stir well.

Combine butter and coffee granules in a small saucepan or skillet. Cook over medium-low heat until butter melts and coffee granules dissolve, stirring occasionally. Remove from heat and let cool to room temperature (don't let butter resolidify).

Combine butter mixture, sugars, egg and egg yolk in a large bowl. Beat at medium speed with an electric mixer until blended. Gradually add flour mixture, beating at low speed just until blended. Stir in mega-chips and walnuts.

Drop dough by heaping tablespoonfuls 2 inches apart onto ungreased baking sheets. Bake at 325 degrees for 12 to 14 minutes. Let cool slightly on baking sheets. Remove to wire racks to cool completely. Makes 20 cookies.

Peanutty Candy Bar Brownies

21-oz. pkg. fudge brownie mix
¼ c. vegetable oil
½ c. creamy peanut butter

3 (7-oz.) peanuts in milk chocolate
   candy bars

These brownies have a gooey center when served warm. The longer they cool, the firmer the candy bar center becomes.

Prepare brownie mix batter according to package directions, using ¼ cup oil instead of ½ cup as package directs. Stir peanut butter into batter. Spread ½ of brownie batter into an ungreased 13"x9" pan. Place whole candy bars across batter. Spread remaining batter over candy bars.

Bake at 350 degrees for 29 minutes. Cool completely on a wire rack. Cut into squares. Makes 3 dozen.

Chewy Almond-Fudge Bars

Coconut candy bars and toasted almonds give this brownie personality. If you like firm bars, chill them.

19.8-oz. pkg. chewy fudge brownie
  mix
3 T. vegetable oil
1 c. sweetened condensed milk
14 miniature chocolate-covered
  coconut candy bars, chopped
  (1¼ cups)

¾ c. chopped natural almonds,
  toasted

Prepare brownie mix according to package directions, reducing vegetable oil to 3 tablespoons; pour into a lightly greased 13"x9" pan. Pour sweetened condensed milk over batter; sprinkle with chopped candy bars and almonds.

Bake at 350 degrees for 36 to 38 minutes. Let cool completely in pan on a wire rack. Cut into bars. Makes 2 dozen.

Merry Cherry Fudge

36 maraschino cherries with
   stems, juice reserved
12-oz. pkg semi-sweet chocolate
   chips
6 (1-oz.) squares bittersweet
   baking chocolate, chopped

14-oz. can sweetened condensed
   milk
1 c. chopped pecans

Lightly coat an 8"x8" pan with vegetable spray; set aside. Blot cherries dry with paper towels.

Combine chocolates in a heavy saucepan; place over very low heat and stir until melted and smooth. Remove from heat, and stir in sweetened condensed milk and reserved one teaspoon cherry juice. Stir in pecans. Spoon mixture into prepared pan. Immediately press cherries into fudge, leaving top of each cherry and stem exposed. Cover and chill fudge 2 hours. Cut fudge into 36 squares. Store in an airtight container in refrigerator. Makes 2 pounds.

This easy fudge recipe has a sweet cherry in every square.

Cookie Dough Truffles

½ c. butter, softened
½ c. brown sugar, packed
¼ c. sugar
¼ c. thawed egg substitute
1 t. vanilla extract
1¼ c. all-purpose flour

1 c. miniature semi-sweet
   chocolate chips
¾ c. chopped pecans or walnuts
12-oz. pkg. semi-sweet chocolate
   chips
1½ T. shortening

Beat butter at medium speed with an electric mixer until creamy; gradually add sugars, beating well. Add egg substitute and vanilla; beat well. Add flour to butter mixture; beat well. Stir in miniature chocolate chips and chopped pecans. Cover and chill 30 minutes.

Shape mixture into one-inch balls. Cover and freeze balls until very firm.

Place 12-ounce package of chips and shortening in a one-quart glass bowl; melt in microwave according to package directions. Using 2 forks, quickly dip frozen truffles into melted chocolate, coating completely. Place on wax paper to harden. Store truffles in refrigerator up to 3 days. Makes 4½ dozen.

This chocolate chip cookie dough comes in candy form wrapped in a chocolate shell.

Goodies for Giving

Page 148

Wrap a few of these
easy-to-make gifts from the
kitchen and get a head start
with homemade holiday goodies.
Some are sweet, some are
savory...but they're all
made with love.

Slice & Bake Sugar Cookies, page 151

Ho-Ho Cocoa Mix

Fill a plastic bag with several servings of this cocoa mix and place in a decorative mug. You can easily double or triple this recipe, and store it in an airtight container up to 2 months.

1½ c. powdered sugar
1½ c. non-fat powdered milk
½ c. baking cocoa

½ c. non-dairy creamer
1½ c. mini marshmallows

Combine all ingredients, stirring well. Store in an airtight container up to 2 months. For each serving, add one cup hot water to ½ cup cocoa mix; stir well. Makes 8 servings.

142

Candy Cane Stirrers

6-oz. pkg. semi-sweet chocolate chips, divided

50 mini peppermint candy canes

Place ¾ cup chocolate chips in a small microwave-safe bowl. Microwave on low power (10%) for 1½ minutes. Stir chocolate until smooth; microwave 20 more seconds, if necessary. Add remaining chocolate and stir until smooth. Set bowl in a pan of hot water to keep chocolate soft, making sure water does not mix with chocolate. Dip straight end of each candy cane into chocolate to coat; lay on wax paper to cool. Wrap each candy cane in clear plastic wrap. Makes 50.

These handy stirrers will hang right on the edge of your favorite mugs.

Christmas Crunch

12-oz. pkg. white chocolate chips
1 c. small pretzels
1 c. apple-cinnamon cereal

1 c. graham cracker cereal
1 c. pecans

Melt white chocolate chips in a saucepan over low heat. Combine pretzels and remaining 3 ingredients in a large bowl and pour melted chocolate chips over mixture, stirring well to coat. Line baking sheet with wax paper; spread mixture on baking sheet and refrigerate. When completely cool, break into pieces and store in airtight containers. Makes 4 cups.

"Layer in tins and it's ready for gift-giving!"
—Mary Lou Traylor
Arlington, TN

Chocolate-Peanut Popcorn

12 c. popped popcorn
2¼ c. salted peanuts
1¾ c. milk chocolate chips

1 c. corn syrup
¼ c. butter or margarine

Combine popcorn and nuts in a greased roasting pan; set aside.
Melt chocolate chips, corn syrup and butter in a heavy saucepan, stirring constantly. Bring mixture to a boil; pour over popcorn, tossing well to coat.
Bake at 300 degrees for 30 to 40 minutes, stirring every 10 minutes. Remove from oven; stir and cool slightly in pan. Remove popcorn to a baking sheet lined with wax paper to cool completely. Store in an airtight container. Makes 14 cups.

Milk chocolate, popcorn and peanuts make this great snack...all you need is a good movie.

Nutty Snack Mix

16-oz. pkg. crisp wheat cereal
   squares
1 lb. pecan halves
16-oz. can cocktail peanuts
13½-oz. pkg. baked snack crackers
12-oz. pkg. corn-and-rice cereal
10-oz. pkg. doughnut-shaped oat
   cereal

6 c. small pretzel twists
2½ c. butter or margarine, melted
¼ c. Worcestershire sauce
2 T. garlic powder
1½ T. onion salt
1½ T. celery salt
½ t. ground red pepper

Combine first 7 ingredients in a large roasting pan or 2 smaller pans. Stir together melted butter and remaining 5 ingredients; pour over cereal mixture and toss well.

Cover and bake at 225 degrees for one hour. Uncover and bake one more hour, stirring occasionally. Cool completely. Store in airtight containers. Makes 42 cups.

Herbal Cheese Spread

2 (8-oz.) pkgs. cream cheese,
   softened
½ c. heavy cream
1 T. olive oil
2 cloves garlic, minced

3 T. fresh parsley, minced
3 T. fresh chives, chopped
⅛ t. fresh thyme
Salt and white pepper to taste

Combine cream cheese and cream, beating at medium speed with an electric mixer until fluffy. Add olive oil and remaining ingredients; stir until thoroughly combined. Spoon into small, decorative containers and cover. Store in refrigerator up to 2 weeks. Makes 2½ cups.

Olive Pesto

(pictured on opposite page)

¾ c. pitted kalamata or black
   olives
½ c. packed fresh flat-leaf parsley
   sprigs
¼ c. packed fresh basil leaves

1 large shallot, chopped
2 cloves garlic, peeled and pressed
3 T. extra-virgin olive oil
¼ c. freshly grated Parmesan
   cheese

Process first 5 ingredients in a blender until minced, stopping to scrape down sides. Add oil and cheese; process until blended. Transfer to a small bowl. Cover and chill, if desired. Store in refrigerator. Makes one cup.

Sun-Dried Tomato & Roasted Garlic Pesto

★ ★ ★

1 whole head of garlic
3 T. extra-virgin olive oil, divided
8½-oz. jar sun-dried tomatoes,
   packed in olive oil
⅓ c. packed fresh flat-leaf
   parsley sprigs

2 T. chopped green onions
2 T. freshly grated Parmesan
   cheese

This pretty pesto is delicious tossed with hot cooked pasta or served as an appetizer on toasted French bread.

Cut top off garlic, leaving head intact. Place garlic on a piece of aluminum foil, cut side up; drizzle with 2 tablespoons olive oil. Wrap in foil and bake at 350 degrees for 40 minutes. Remove from oven and cool. Discard outermost layer of papery skin from garlic. Scoop out soft garlic pulp with a small spoon or knife. Place roasted garlic, sun-dried tomatoes, parsley and green onions in a blender or food processor; process until finely minced. Add remaining one tablespoon oil and cheese; process until blended. Transfer to a small bowl; cover and chill. Makes 1¼ cups.

Hot Jalapeño Jam

12 large jalapeño peppers, halved
  and seeded
2 large tomatoes, peeled and
  chopped
1 onion, finely chopped

1 Granny Smith apple, cored and
  grated
½ c. red wine vinegar
⅔ c. sugar
½ t. pepper

   Broil peppers, cut side down, on an aluminum foil-lined baking sheet 3 inches from heat about 15 minutes or until peppers look blistered. Place peppers in a large plastic freezer zipping bag; seal and let stand 10 minutes to loosen skins. Peel and chop peppers.
   Combine jalapeño peppers, tomatoes, onion and remaining ingredients in a large saucepan. Place over medium heat; cook, stirring constantly, until sugar dissolves. Bring to a boil; reduce heat and simmer, uncovered, 30 minutes. Spoon into hot sterilized jars, filling to ¼ inch from top. Wipe jar rims. Cover at once with metal lids and screw on bands. Cool completely. Store in refrigerator up to one month. Makes 3 cups.

Go-Team Chili Seasoning

Give this seasoning mix with a stack of soup bowls or a new soup pot . . . just right for those cold, winter days.

2 T. dried minced onion
1 T. all-purpose flour
1½ t. chili powder
1 t. salt

1 t. sugar
½ t. garlic powder
½ t. ground red pepper
½ t. cumin

   Mix all ingredients together; store in an airtight container. Attach a tag with instructions. Makes ¼ cup.

Chili Instructions:
Brown one pound ground beef in a skillet; drain. Add seasoning mix, 2 (15½-ounce) cans kidney beans and 2 (16-ounce) cans stewed tomatoes. Reduce heat; simmer 10 minutes, stirring occasionally. Makes 4 to 6 servings.

Wild Rice & Mushroom Soup Mix

Present soup mix in a pretty fabric bag and tie with raffia.

2 (¾-oz.) pkgs. country gravy mix
1½ T. chicken bouillon granules
2 t. dried minced onion
2 t. dried celery flakes

1 t. dried parsley
¼ c. instant wild rice, uncooked
1 c. instant rice, uncooked
2 T. dried mushrooms, chopped

   Pour gravy mix into a one-pint, wide-mouth jar. Combine bouillon granules, onion, celery and parsley in a small bowl; pour over gravy mix. Layer with rice and mushrooms; seal lid. Attach a tag with instructions.

Empty jar into a large saucepan. Add 7 cups water; bring to a boil. Reduce heat, cover and simmer 25 to 30 minutes until rice is tender, stirring occasionally. Makes 6 servings.

Quick & Easy Pancake Mix

10 c. all-purpose flour
2½ c. powdered milk
½ c. sugar

¼ c. baking powder
1½ T. salt

Combine all ingredients in a large bowl; blend well. Place in a large container or divide by 2-cup amounts into plastic zipping bags. Store in a cool, dry place for up to 8 months. Attach a tag with instructions. Makes 12 cups.

Pancake Instructions:
Combine 2 cups mix, one beaten egg and 1¼ cups water or milk until just moistened; drop by ¼ cupfuls onto a greased, hot griddle or skillet. Cook pancakes until tops are covered with bubbles and edges look cooked; turn and cook other side. Makes 12 to 14 pancakes.

★ ★ ★

Pair Quick & Easy Pancake Mix with jars of fruit-flavored syrups for a yummy breakfast-time gift.

Candied Fruit Loaf

2 c. all-purpose flour
¾ c. sugar
4 t. baking powder
¼ t. salt
½ t. cinnamon
¼ c. chopped red candied pineapple
¼ c. chopped red candied cherries
¼ c. currants

¼ c. chopped almonds, toasted
¼ c. chopped pecans, toasted
2 T. chopped candied lemon peel
2 eggs
1 c. milk
¼ c. butter or margarine, melted
1 t. vanilla extract
¼ c. bourbon (optional)

Combine first 5 ingredients in a large bowl. Stir in pineapple and next 5 ingredients. Whisk together eggs and next 3 ingredients. Add egg mixture to flour mixture; stir until well blended. Spoon batter into a lightly greased 8"x4" loaf pan.

Bake at 325 degrees for 1 hour and 5 minutes or until a toothpick inserted in center comes out clean. Cool in pan on a wire rack 5 minutes. Remove from pan; cool completely on wire rack. If desired, soak cheesecloth in ¼ cup bourbon, wrap around cake and place in an airtight container; refrigerate 4 to 10 days. Makes 10 servings.

Eggnog Cakes

These tasty little treats begin with a mix and are made extra-special with eggnog, pecans and a powdered sugar glaze. They're a special way to send holiday greetings to friends.

½ c. pecans, finely chopped
18¼-oz. pkg. yellow cake mix
1 c. eggnog
¼ c. vegetable oil
3 eggs

2 T. orange juice
¼ t. nutmeg
2 c. powdered sugar
6 T. orange juice

Sprinkle 2 teaspoons chopped pecans into each of 9 generously greased and floured mini Bundt® pans; set aside.

Combine cake mix and next 5 ingredients in a large bowl; beat at medium speed with an electric mixer 2 minutes. Pour batter evenly into prepared pans.

Bake at 350 degrees for 25 minutes or until a toothpick inserted in center comes out clean. Cool in pans on wire racks 10 to 15 minutes; remove from pans and cool on wire racks.

Combine powdered sugar and 6 tablespoons orange juice in a small bowl; stir well. Drizzle glaze evenly over cakes. Makes 9 mini cakes.

This recipe can also be made into one large cake. You'll need a 12-cup Bundt® pan and then follow the directions above, sprinkling all the pecans into a well-greased and floured pan. Proceed as directed; then bake at 350 degrees for 35 minutes or until a long wooden toothpick inserted in center of cake comes out clean. Makes 14 servings.

Apple Cobbler in a Jar

Ascorbic-acid powder (we tested
  with Fruit Fresh)
5 to 6 lbs. cooking apples (about
  18 c.)
4½ c. sugar
1 c. cornstarch

2 t. cinnamon
1 t. salt
¼ t. nutmeg
10 c. water
3 T. lemon juice

Prepare ascorbic-acid solution according to manufacturer's directions; set
aside. Peel and slice apples. Drop apple slices into ascorbic-acid solution.
(Allow to stand in solution only 20 minutes.)

Combine sugar and next 6 ingredients in a Dutch oven. Cook over medium-
high heat 15 minutes or until thick and bubbly, stirring frequently. Keep filling
hot. Alternately pack 3 cups raw apples and 2 cups filling into 6 hot 1-quart
jars, filling to ½ inch from top. Remove air bubbles; wipe jar rims. Cover at once
with metal lids and screw on bands. Process in boiling-water bath 25 minutes.
Makes 6 quarts.

Apple Cobbler

1 qt. jar Apple Cobbler in a Jar
9-inch pie crust, unbaked
1 egg yolk

1 t. water
1 T. cinnamon sugar

Pour Apple Cobbler in a Jar into an ungreased 9" pie plate. Place pie crust
over filling; fold edges under and crimp. Cut slits in top for steam to escape.

Combine egg yolk and water. Brush crust with egg mixture; sprinkle with
cinnamon sugar. Bake at 400 degrees for 30 minutes or until golden. Cover
with aluminum foil after 20 minutes to prevent excessive browning. Makes
one cobbler.

*Welcome new neighbors
with a quart of cobbler
in a jar. The work is
all done except for
the baking...and the
sharing.*

Christmas Truffles

⅔ c. heavy cream
12 oz. pkg. semi-sweet chocolate
   chips
4 T. unsalted butter, softened
Toasted flaked coconut

Toasted finely chopped nuts
Powdered sugar
Chocolate sprinkles
Baking cocoa
Candy paper baking cups

Heat cream just to a boil in a medium saucepan. Remove from heat and
whisk in chocolate chips and butter; beat until smooth. Place pan over a bowl
of ice water. Beat at medium speed with an electric mixer 3 to 4 minutes or
until soft peaks form. Cover and refrigerate 3 hours or until firm.
   Scoop out one-inch balls using a melon baller or small scoop. Dip balls into
various coatings; roll between your hands. Place in paper cups or on a sheet
of wax paper. Cover and store in refrigerator. Makes about 3½ dozen.

Slice & Bake Sugar Cookies

(pictured on page 141)

2 c. butter or margarine, softened
2 c. sugar
3 eggs
2 t. vanilla extract

1 t. lemon extract
6 c. all-purpose flour
1 t. baking soda
½ t. cinnamon

Give rolls of sugar cookies with decorations included. Yummy chocolate-dipped raisins, sparkly sugar and sprinkles make cookie baking fun! You can make and freeze these gift logs of dough up to a month before delivering them.

Cream butter and 2 cups sugar in a large bowl until fluffy. Add eggs and flavorings; beat until smooth. Combine flour, baking soda and cinnamon. Gradually stir dry ingredients into creamed mixture; stir until a soft dough forms. Divide dough into 4 equal portions; roll each portion into a 10-inch log. Wrap each log in plastic wrap and freeze. Wrap each frozen log in aluminum foil and again in printed fabric, if desired. Attach a tag with baking instructions. Makes 4 rolls (each yielding 3 dozen cookies).

Baking Instructions:

Store dough in refrigerator up to 5 days (or freeze up to one month). When ready to bake, cut chilled dough into ¼-inch slices; place on greased baking sheets. Sprinkle evenly with sugar. Bake at 350 degrees for 10 to 12 minutes. Remove to wire racks to cool. Makes 3 dozen.

Cranberry Lemon Vinegar

1 qt. white wine vinegar
½ c. sweetened dried cranberries
1½ t. grated lemon zest
6 sprigs fresh thyme

Additional fresh thyme sprigs
  (optional)

Combine vinegar, cranberries and lemon zest in a large non-aluminum saucepan. Bring to a boil over medium-high heat. Transfer mixture to a heat-proof nonmetal container; add 6 thyme sprigs. Cover and let stand in refrigerator one week to let flavors blend.

Pour mixture through a wire-mesh strainer into a bowl, discarding solids. Transfer to hot sterilized gift bottles. Add additional thyme sprigs, if desired. Seal with a cork or other airtight lid. Store in refrigerator up to one week with herbs or up to one month with no herbs. Makes 3¾ cups.

Packaging Pizzazz

•Make a gift bag with a window to show off your sweets. Just cut a shape from the front of a small sack and glue cellophane or plastic wrap on the inside to cover the opening. Then fill the sack with goodies.

•Stamp a child's handprint onto a plain potholder, using fabric paint. Attach potholder to bag of baked goods with ribbon and give to grandparents.

•Splatterpaint a cardboard bakery box using toothbrush bristles and red and green paint. Fill box with tissue paper, and tuck in a homemade pie, candies or cookies.

Recipe Index

Helpful Holiday Hints

Holiday Countdown
*There's so much fun to be had between
Thanksgiving and Christmas...these reminders and
planning tips will help you fit it all in.*

In November

• **Start baking holiday cookies and cakes.** You can freeze them (if they're unfrosted) for several months.

• **Purchase cranberries** while they're readily available at the local supermarket. They keep well in the freezer and come in handy for recipes and decorating.

• **Take stock of seasonal items,** such as holiday dinnerware and glasses, serving pieces and Christmas decorations, to see what needs to be purchased or cleaned.

• **Update your Christmas card list** and address envelopes.

• **Line up babysitters** for special events.

In December

• **Clip greenery for decorations.** To make the greenery stay fresh longer, soak cut branches in water for at least 24 hours before adding to arrangements.

• **Stock the pantry** for spur-of-the-moment snacks and to avoid last-minute dashes to the grocery store for recipe ingredients.

• **Put up wreaths and garlands mid-month.** Mist the greenery every few days to keep it fresh and green.

• **If ordering gifts by mail,** order the first week of December to ensure arrival by Christmas.

• **Mail Christmas cards** and packages early in the month.

Party-Ready Cupboard

Here's a quick checklist of pantry staples to have on hand during the holidays.

- [ ] Assorted nuts
- [ ] Baking basics: flour, sugar, baking powder and baking soda
- [ ] Baking chocolate
- [ ] Butter
- [ ] Canned chicken broth
- [ ] Canned pumpkin
- [ ] Coffee (both regular and flavored) and tea
- [ ] Cranberries
- [ ] Eggnog
- [ ] Flaked coconut
- [ ] Frozen pie shells
- [ ] Hot cocoa
- [ ] Jams, jellies and preserves
- [ ] Semi-sweet chips
- [ ] Sodas
- [ ] Spices: ground allspice, cinnamon, cloves, ginger and nutmeg
- [ ] Sweetened condensed milk
- [ ] Whipping cream

Thoughtful Gifts for Special Friends

• Make your own personal Christmas cards or stationery using rubber stamps and heavy construction paper. Bundle several cards together and tie with a ribbon to give as a gift.

• Tuck favorite family recipes in a basket with new kitchen towels.

• Record your children singing Christmas carols and send tapes to relatives who live far away.

• Give someone a gift certificate promising you'll teach them a skill that you do well. If you plan to teach how to embroider, for example, include needles, hoop, fabric and patterns.

• Organize family photos and children's artwork in a scrapbook for a grandparent.

Favorite Holiday Recipes

Appetizers & Beverages.......

....

....

....

Entrées ....

....

....

....

Sides & Salads ....

....

....

....

Cookies & Candies ....

....

....

....

Desserts ....

....

....

....

Entertaining Planner

*Use these pages to jot down the details that will help you relax
& enjoy all your holiday party plans.*

Treats for Instant Entertaining
Keep these items on hand for unexpected guests.

• **Keep ready-to-eat carrot and celery sticks in the refrigerator.** With a veggie dip or salad dressing, they make an easy snack or appetizer.

• **Set out cream cheese and preserves** as spreads for an assortment of crackers.

• **Bake and freeze muffins up to one month ahead.** Reheat in the toaster oven or microwave.

• **Store a container of cut-up brownies in the freezer.** For a quick dessert, pop brownies into the microwave, and then top with vanilla ice cream and hot fudge sauce.

• **Wrap a cheesecake in heavy-duty plastic wrap,** or place it in an airtight container; it will keep in the freezer up to one month. Freezing will not harm the flavor or texture. Thaw in refrigerator.

• **Brew coffee with strips of orange peel** for added flavor. Offer with sugar cubes, whipped cream, grated chocolate and cinnamon-stick stirrers.

Time-Saving Make-Ahead Tips
Save time in the kitchen with these suggestions.

• **When browning ground beef, brown extra** to have on hand for quick meal preparation. Freeze it in freezer zipping bags in pound or half-pound portions. It will keep in the freezer up to three months.

• **Chop green pepper or onion ahead of time for holiday cooking.** Freeze it in freezer zipping bags up to three months.

• **Freeze extra sauce, gravy or broth in ice-cube trays;** reheat the cubes as needed or drop into simmering soups and stews.

• **When you're shredding cheese for a recipe,** shred extra to freeze for later use.

• **Freeze leftover veggies** to be combined for homemade vegetable soup.

Party To-Do List
*Make plans here for shopping, cooking and decorating so the day of
your party will be carefree.*

·   ·

·   ·

·   ·

·   ·

·   ·

·   ·

·   ·

·   ·

·   ·

·   ·

Guest List
List names to make sure you don't miss anyone.

Last-Minute Details
Use this space as a final checklist before the party.

Christmas Dinner Planner

*Here are some tips that will help
as you plan your holiday meal.*

Top Ideas for Terrific Tables

*These centerpiece ideas are quick and easy,
and many use items that you already
have around the house.*

• **Fill bowls with colorful ornaments,** and arrange them down the center of the table.

• **Cluster a collection of candles** in the center of the table. Tuck in sprigs of greenery and berries among the candles.

• **Stack two glass cake stands,** and fill them with greenery and citrus fruit for a colorful accent. Add ribbon to match your decorating scheme.

• **To add height, light and dimension to your table,** place pillar candles in clear glass vases, and fill in around the bottom of the candles with glass beads.

• **Pair inexpensive goblets painted with a Christmassy pattern** with white china for an easy holiday table setting.

• **Enhance a simple centerpiece** made of evergreen foliage clipped from your yard by placing a mirror underneath. Arrange glittery ornaments at the base of the container.

• **Add a charger plate to traditional china** for a festive update. Usually 12 inches in diameter, chargers are placed underneath dinner plates to create a border around the plate. Gold or silver chargers blend with a variety of china patterns.

Getting Ready For the Meal

*Plan ahead for the big Christmas dinner,
and focus on enjoying friends and family.*

• **Clean out** your refrigerator and freezer to make room for all those holiday goodies.

• **Start the day with an empty dishwasher,** and you'll find the task of cleanup more manageable.

• **Designate an area** for coffee, tea, juices, water and any other beverages. Your family and friends can serve themselves…this will make them feel right at home.

• **Set the table and select the serving dishes** the day before so on the day of the meal you can attend to just food and family.

Dinner Menu Ideas

Remember to include some family-favorite recipes.

Dinner To-Do List

Write your list here to minimize last-minute surprises.

Family Holiday Memories

Write down memorable moments to enjoy for years to come.

How Did Gooseberry Patch Get Started?

You may know the story of Gooseberry Patch...the tale of two country friends who decided one day over the backyard fence to try their hands at the mail order business. Started in JoAnn's kitchen back in 1984, Vickie & JoAnn's dream of a "Country Store in Your Mailbox" has grown and grown to a 96-page catalog with over 400 products, including cookie cutters, Santas, snowmen, gift baskets, angels and our very own line of cookbooks! What an adventure for two country friends!

Through our catalogs and books, Gooseberry Patch has met country friends from all over the world. While sharing letters and phone calls, we found that our friends love to cook, decorate, garden and craft. We've created Kate, Holly & Mary Elizabeth to represent these devoted friends who live and love the country lifestyle the way we do. They're just like you & me... they're our "Country Friends®!"

Your friends at Gooseberry Patch

Kate ★ Holly ★ Mary Elizabeth ★ Spot